WALKING
in the LIGHT

WALKING *in the* LIGHT

A Jewish-Christian Vision of Healing and Wholeness

Bruce G. Epperly
Lewis D. Solomon

CHALICE
PRESS
ST. LOUIS, MISSOURI

Cover art: © GettyImages
Cover and interior design: Elizabeth Wright

This book is printed on acid-free, recycled paper.

Visit Chalice Press on the World Wide Web at
www.chalicepress.com

10 9 8 7 6 5 4 3 2 1   04 05 06 07 08 09

Library of Congress Cataloging–in–Publication Data

Epperly, Bruce Gordon.
  Walking in the light : a Jewish-Christian vision of healing and wholeness / Bruce G. Epperly, Lewis D. Solomon.
    p. cm.
  Includes bibliographical references.
  ISBN 0-8272-4249-2 (pbk. : alk. paper)
  1. Healing—Religious aspects—Christianity. 2. Healing—Religious aspects—Judaism. 3. Christianity and other religions—Judaism. 4. Judaism—Relations—Christianity. I. Solomon, Lewis D. II. Title.
  BT732.E68 2004
  248.4—dc22

                                                    2004008673

Printed in the United States of America

Contents

*We dedicate this book to
spiritual and life partners,
Katherine Gould Epperly and
Janet Stern Solomon*

A Word of Thanks

We exist in an intricate ecology of relationships that weaves together mind, body, spirit, and persons and their social contexts. Healing and wholeness arise out of our experience of relatedness with the gentle movements of the Holy Adventure, embodied in friends and family. Life in its fullness is grounded in the gratitude that comes from affirming and embracing the graceful love we have received through the years.

We would, above all, like to thank our wives, Katherine Gould Epperly and Janet Stern Solomon. They have been spiritual partners, supporters, and inspirations to excellence in our work. I, Bruce, am grateful for the encouragement of my son Matthew and mother-in-law Maxine Gould, as well as a handful of friends who believed in the importance of this project and prayed for its successful completion.

We are grateful to Rabbi Harold White, who has embodied the spirit of Shalom in his three decades of leadership in Jewish-Christian relationships and interfaith dialogue. We are also grateful to David Polk for his support and gentle editorial work. I, Bruce, am thankful for David's editorial support since 1991 and his commitment to quality work in process-relational theology.

We also thank the members of the Palisades Community Church in Washington D.C., who invited us to share early drafts of our first book *Mending the World* as well as this and a future text to be published by Chalice Press.

CHAPTER ONE

Raising the Light

Once upon a time, according to the sixteenth-century Jewish mystic Rabbi Isaac Luria, God lived in solitary splendor. God's radiance filled the entire universe. In the Divine imagination, the vision of a world of wondrous beauty took form. Filled with love for the world that was to come into being, the Divine Artist imagined creatures who would be fellow artists in this new creation. When God began to create the universe, the Divine—like the good parent—withdrew from a portion of infinite space, leaving a vacuum for future creativity and freedom to emerge. Into that generous void, Divine light burst forth in splendor and radiated across the newly formed universe, channeling through the vessels God had created to mediate this holy light to the emerging world. The energy was so intense at that moment of Divine creativity that some of the vessels shattered, trapping the individual sparks in the fragments of the shattered vessels. From that moment on, creation would both reveal and conceal God's radiant wisdom. Though the sparks were still connected with their Creator, they forgot their spiritual identity and eternal unity with God and their cosmic companions. Creaturely freedom and creativity would now bring forth both beauty and ugliness, love and hate, health and sickness.

In this lively and ambiguous world, we have been given a holy vocation. Our task as God's children is to discover the Divine spark in ourselves and enable each of our companion sparks to discover her or his true identity as a child of God. In raising the light from the darkness and reminding each spark of its Divine origin, we become God's partners in mending the world and ushering in the age of wholeness and peace. Partners with Divine creativity, we bring healing to ourselves and the world around us.

Nearly 1,500 years before Rabbi Luria, the author of the gospel of John proclaimed a similar vision of the creative power of God and the role of humankind in the transformation of the universe. Invoking the radiant images of the creation story of Genesis, the first chapter of John's gospel described the universe as the creation of Divine Wisdom and Light. All things are created by the Divine Light whose living Word echoes ceaselessly throughout the universe. Even the deepest darkness reveals the Light of the World. To this early Christian sage, the Wisdom and Word of God has a home in human flesh, enlightening all things through the light revealed in Jesus of Nazareth. In the Divine "Word made flesh," humans discover their true humanity and responsibility as cocreators with the Divine Parent.

> All things came into being through [the Divine Word], and without [the Divine Word] not one thing came into being. What has come into being in [the Divine Word] was life, and the life was the light of all people. The light shines in the darkness, and the darkness did not overcome it...The true light, which enlightens everyone, was coming into the world. (Jn. 1:3–5, 9)

In the spirit of the Hebraic tradition, the healer of Nazareth—the embodiment of God's own healing light—proclaimed to his followers, "You are the light of the world" (Mt. 5:14) and challenged them to see God's light in the most unexpected places—foreigners, outcasts, oppressors, persons of dubious morality or with serious illnesses, and in their own imperfect lives. In a world of darkness, Jesus, like the Hebraic sages before him, preached that God's true light shines within everyone. In letting our light shine like a beacon on a hilltop, we raise the Divine light in others, enabling them to claim their own birthright as children of God's light. As later Christian sages were to proclaim, the Divine became human in order to raise humankind toward divinity. God entered the world of flesh so that embodiment might become holy. This was not God's first or only entry into our world. The light that burst forth in Bethlehem revealed the Holy Light that was present in God's creation of the universe, the birth of each child, and the wisdom of the Hebraic prophets and sages of all lands throughout the ages.

Partnership with God

In our earlier book *Mending the World*, we shared the story of Michelangelo and the boulder.[1] When the sculptor was asked why he was pounding on a jagged rock, he responded with the words, "There's an angel inside, and I'm trying to let it out." Judaism and Christianity are profoundly life-affirming faiths. Our bodies and the planet were created by God's overflowing love. God's Wisdom permeates all things, including life's boulders. The world is full of God's presence and is, in its essence, "very good" (Gen. 1:1–31). God constantly seeks to bring forth the angelic beauty hidden within each creature. As Jewish mysticism proclaims, around every blade of grass angels chant, "Grow, grow." The Divine *Shekinah*, the indwelling presence of God, seeks to make the whole creation the conscious dwelling place of the Holy One.

Jewish and Christian spirituality proclaims the miraculous nature of life. According to Rabbi Abraham Joshua Heschel, "Hidden miracles are the basis for the entire Torah. A [person] has no share in the Torah unless he [or she] knows that all things and all events in the life of the individual as well as society are miracles."[2] The writers of the Psalms saw holiness in the stars above and the intricacy of human embodiment. Jesus saw holiness in little children, the lilies of the field, and the birds of the air. We can find holiness in checking our e-mail, driving our children to piano lessons, volunteering in a soup kitchen or legal aid society, sharing a meal with our spouse, or taking our medication.

According to Jewish and Christian mystics, we live in a God-breathed universe, in which the Divine Spirit touches and enlivens all things. God's love gives birth to each moment and each creature. God inspires every quest for truth and healing in our pluralistic age. God is the soul of the universe, whose wisdom still radiates in all things, creating sparks of beauty wherever it touches.

Jewish wisdom proclaims that each of the 600,000 Jews present for God's revelation of the Torah at Mount Sinai heard God speak in a unique and personal voice. God's revelation to humankind is diverse, plural, and personal. It comes to us, addressing our deepest joys and gravest concerns. It aims at the unique healing that will bring us joy and enable our light to shine brightly.

The infinite Soul of the Universe is the intimate companion of each creature. God's love creates the universe, but also receives the gift of our lives. The philosopher Alfred North Whitehead describes God as "the fellow sufferer who understands." In that same spirit, Rabbi Abraham Joshua Heschel speaks of God's relationship to the world in terms of the Divine pathos. The Holy One experiences our lives in their entirety and shares in the pain of each divine spark in exile. God feels the ecstasy of the mystic, the passion of young lovers, the freedom of a child playing, and the laughter of friends. But, God also experiences the anxiety at hospital room, the doubt of those who question God's existence in the wake of tragedy, and the despair of a mother helplessly watching her child die of starvation. Wherever we are, God is with us, seeking constantly to bring order out of chaos and healing from pain. Our lives go forth from the matrix of Divine Creativity and return to the Beauty from which we have come. As Christian philosopher Charles Hartshorne asserts:

> The all inclusiveness of the world-mind, [is] not that it is exalted above suffering, but that no pain or joy is beneath its notice…Our deliberate acts set up currents, as it were, in the mind of God, as the adrenaline in our brain will set up currents in our human minds. Each of us is a pulse in the Eternal Mind.[3]

We matter to God and we matter to the universe. Jewish and Christian spirituality alike see our world as unfinished and full of possibility. Creation continues moment by moment. In the pulse of creation, God is always doing a new thing. But, God needs our companionship and sacred deeds (*mitzvoth* in Hebrew) to bring forth the fullness of Divine Beauty in our world. We are God's partners and cocreators in liberating the light from the darkness. In words that describe Judaism, but are equally applicable to Christianity, Heschel asserts that:

> There is only one way to define the Jewish religion. It is the awareness of God's interest in [humankind]. Our task is to concern ourselves with this interest, to carry out His vision of our task. God is in need of [us] for the attainment of His ends…Life is a partnership of God and [humankind].[4]

God needs our creativity and adventurous love to promote the healing and evolution of our world, just as we need God's guidance and support to find our way in the intricate maze of life.

A Guide for the Perplexed

The Hebraic patriarch Jacob once dreamed of a ladder connecting heaven and earth. Angels descended to earth from the ladder. With each angelic footstep, God's words of promise echoed in the darkness. When he awakened, Jacob exclaimed, "Surely [God] is in this place—and I did not know it" (Gen. 28:16). This is our story as well. The universe is permeated with Divinity. Our bodies as well as our minds reveal the brush strokes of the Divine Artist. As we, like Jacob, face the wonder and woundedness of our lives, God promises inspiration as well as challenge for the journey ahead. "Angels," reflecting the diverse media through which God communicates with us, are constantly coming to our aid whenever we feel alone and perplexed.

Every cell of our bodies reveals Divine wisdom. Yet, we may fail to see the holiness of the moment and the Divine resources that are at our fingertips. The Divine Presence is often hidden from our eyes by the pain of the world and the everyday stresses of our own lives. We doubt that God could be a healing presence in Auschwitz and in the falling of the Twin Towers. But, closer to home, we wonder if we can find traces of Divinity in a diagnosis of a life-threatening or chronic illness. In such moments, Isaac Luria's image of the shattering of the primordial light seems to describe our own experience: The light of God is hidden and imprisoned in the husks of darkness and ignorance. Confronted by tragedy and suffering, we struggle with the questions, "Is God in this situation? Does God really care about persons in pain? Can God do anything to heal the suffering of the world? Can something of beauty come from this tragedy?"

Still, within the darkness, persons of faith believe that the Divine Light shines, and affirm that the hope of the world depends on seeing this holy light and bringing it forth wherever it may be found. As John's gospel boldly affirms, "The light shines in the darkness, and the darkness did not overcome it" (Jn. 1:5). In our quest to see the light in life's challenges, we are confronted by the Divine Inquisitor who asks, "What will you do to transform the world? Will you play your unique role in mending the universe?"

Mending the world takes place in the cosmos as a whole, and in every individual life. As Rabbi Lawrence Kushner notes, "Everyone and everything is latent with holiness, awaiting our touch."[5] In raising even one spark to its Divine nature, we are saving the world. We are God's healing touch in the present moment, aiding God's desire to bring forth abundant life for all creation.

Progressive Judaism and Christianity affirm that all creation participates in a holy adventure. The great stories of Judaism and Christianity—the creation of the universe, the call of Moses, and the cross of Jesus—as well as the stories of humankind's ongoing fidelity to God and the world—the lively mysticism of the Baal Shem Tov (who brought new life to Jewish spirituality), the nonviolent quest for justice of Mahatma Gandhi and Martin Luther King, and the unconditional compassion Mother Teresa of Calcutta—invite us to recognize God's Holy Adventure in our unique time. We are the messengers of God to our world. We need healing and we are challenged to bring healing to others. God is in this place and we can experience the Holy One right now!

Still, there are times when the world becomes radically off balance and discordant. Often pain and alienation seem more apparent than the love of God. At such moments, God needs our support to bring order out of our own chaos in the Divine quest for harmony. As one Jewish mystic notes, our vocation is to be God's chiropractors, whose task is to bring health and harmony to the universe by aligning ourselves and others with Divine Wisdom. Our calling is personal and intimate, but also cosmic, in scope.

As you explore the chapters ahead, we invite you to become God's partner in healing the world one moment at a time. In the spirit of the Jewish philosopher Maimonides we seek to provide *A Guide for the Perplexed,* whose wisdom enables persons to see God's holy light within the disruptive moments of sickness as well as the joyful moments of health. But, as God's cocreators, we are equally concerned with promoting health and preventing illness through a commitment to spiritual practices, habits of wholeness, and the creation of an environment of health and justice.

Today, we need creative spiritual images to inspire the task of raising God's light amid the shadows of personal and collective pain and disorientation. Too often spirituality has been identified with punishment and sickness rather than healing and forgiveness. Rabbi Mordecai Kaplan notes that "the past has a vote, but not a veto" in the evolution of our spiritual journeys and faith traditions. Judaism and Christianity alike need life-transforming images of God and humankind that embrace both light and darkness, and enable us to respond creatively to the ever-present realities of sickness and pain.

In facing our deepest personal and global challenges, mainstream Judaism and Christianity have often suffered from a failure of imagination and a lack of trust in Divine Creativity. Dwindling memberships and lack of passion in worship are symptoms of our inability to "taste and see" the goodness of God and our failure to envisage lively images of God and provide spiritual practices that enable persons to experience the living God in the adventures of ordinary life.

Our images of God and spiritual practices need greater stature and inclusiveness in order to embrace the pluralism of the world and the complexity of our own experience. Our traditions need to claim the light residing in their own rituals and beliefs so that we may raise the hidden light of world, especially in the dim recesses of sickness, death, and bereavement. As the Rabbi of Rizhen replied to a troubled student:

> When a man walks through the woods on a dark night,
> and for a time another joins him, lantern in hand, but
> at the crossroads they part, the first must grope on his
> way alone. But if a man carries his own light with him
> he need not be afraid of any darkness.[6]

The light is always with us, and healing is just a moment away, but we need to claim its radiance in our lives and religious communities.

In the personal and global complexities of our time, progressive Jews and Christians need to walk together as partners in the quest for God's ultimate healing, Shalom. We need to share our pain at the alienation of the past and claim our hopes for future transformation. Faced with the suffering that surrounds us as well as our personal limitations, we cannot claim to have all the answers. But, we can glimpse enough truth together to guide our footsteps on the journey toward the healing of ourselves, our religious traditions, and our planet. As Rabbi Hayyim counseled his students in preparation for Yom Kippur, the Day of Atonement and Transformation:

> A man lost his way in a great forest. After a while another lost his way and chanced upon the first. Without knowing what had happened to him, he asked the way out of the woods. "I don't know," said the first. "But I can point out the ways that lead further into the thicket, and after that let us try to find the way together."

Rabbi Hayyim concluded his parable with the words, "So, congregation, let us look for the way together."[7]

Today, progressive Christians and Jews need to look for the way to wholeness and healing in partnership with one another. Our historical and theological differences are eclipsed by our common spiritual tradition and commitments. While we affirm that "the whole earth is full of [God's] glory" (Isa. 6:3), we stand humbly before the infinity of the universe, the mystery of human life, and the God who transcends every spiritual image. We affirm that our own bodies, even at the cellular level, reflect this same beauty and wholeness. This universal aim at wholeness is the gentle force in the healing of every wound, the lifting of grief, and the strength to face chronic illness and adversity with hope and courage.

Healing can occur in any circumstance, because God is the source of abundance and new life in all things. Even when no physical cure is possible, we can experience a peace that enables us to face life's most difficult challenges with a sense of hope and equanimity. When a cure is no longer sought, and death and disability are on the horizon, there is always the possibility of spiritual healing when we open ourselves to God's movements in our lives.

We can claim God's fullness in our lives, precisely because the Divine's bias toward healing and reconciliation resides in all things. As Rabbi Kalonymus Kalman affirmed:

> I have heard from the wisest of my teachers, that when a holy person journeys from one place to another, then the Name of the Holy One goes before him [to help him] scout out the right path.[8]

The earliest Christians called themselves the "people of the way." They affirmed the traditions of their Jewish parents who saw faith more as a way of life than a set of creeds to affirm. They saw wholeness as the path of life, embracing body, mind, spirit, and relationships.

Today, as the children of the prophets, healers, and mystics of Judaism and Christianity, we are also pilgrims whose path is cosmic as well as personal. Our path leads through the integration of spirituality and Western medicine, contemplation and healthy exercise, complementary medicine and medical technology, personal well-being and global justice. In the path ahead, we will explore the vision of a healing God and practical ways to experience God as a partner in promoting wholeness and responding to disease.

As we claim God's healing presence in our own lives, we will be inspired to support God's quest to heal the world. In the journey ahead, God goes before us, guiding and inspiring us to raise the healing light in the shadows of sickness, stress, and fatigue. Let us find the way together.

CHAPTER TWO

Healing for the Whole Person

Is That All There Is?

At age forty, Tom faced much more than a midlife crisis. He had risen to the top of his profession. His services as an advertising executive were in high demand. Although he had been married a decade and loved his wife, Susan, his career was the true center of his life. Some weeks he hardly saw Susan except to give her a good-night kiss or accompany her on the many weekend business-related events that dominated their schedule.

Despite his professional success, something had been gnawing at Tom for weeks. He felt growing emotional and physical uneasiness, chronic fatigue, and the feeling that something was missing in his life. He tried to deaden his physical and emotional discomfort by investing himself even more in his work and by drinking an extra cocktail before dinner each night. But still the uneasiness remained. At first, he rationalized it away, "It's just turning forty. Everything starts to break down. I'll get over it." But, he didn't get over it! As the weeks went by, he slowly began to realize that something might truly be wrong in his life. His intuition was confirmed two weeks later by those dreaded words, "You have cancer."

At that moment, Tom's carefully structured world collapsed. Although his physician indicated that the medical prognosis was favorable, Tom plunged into a deep depression. To him, cancer meant only death and disability, and there was no escape from its terrifying grip. Tom kept the diagnosis entirely to himself for nearly a week as he reflected on the imagined future that lay ahead of him—surgery, chemotherapy, hair loss, and eventually death. Although he was not religious, Tom wondered, "Am I being punished for something I've done? Is cancer God's way of getting back at me for neglecting my marriage and spiritual life? Is this some kind of cosmic wake-up call? If so, thanks a lot, God!"

With the possibility of death on the horizon, Tom was troubled by the values that had dominated his life before the diagnosis. "Is professional success all there is to life? Isn't there more to life than work, financial security, retirement, and then death? Isn't there more to marriage than a big house and lavish parties?" For the first time in years, Tom reflected on his childhood faith and the lessons he had learned in Sunday school. He remembered Jesus' story of a wealthy farmer who built a great barn in order to store his riches, only to die on the night it was completed. "Was this going to be the story of my life as well? Gaining the world, but losing my soul?"

Susan was shocked when Tom declared on Sunday morning, "I've decided to skip my golf date. I'm going to church. Right now, I feel lost and need some direction in my life. Maybe, I can find it there." That morning the words of the scripture struck Tom to the core. He heard the story of Jesus' words to a man who been paralyzed for thirty-eight years, "Do you want to be made well?" In his imagination, Tom saw the scene and heard Jesus speaking directly to him, "Tom, do you really want to be healed? And, if so, what are you going to do about it?" That day, Tom remembered the Hebraic wisdom that the early followers of Jesus embraced, "I have set before you life and death, blessings and curses. Choose life" (Deut. 30:19). As he sat quietly in the pew that morning, Tom resolved that from then on he would choose life in all its fullness.

When he returned home from church, Tom finally told Susan about the cancer. With tears in his eyes, he began to tell her all the things that he had buried in his heart throughout their marriage. He begged her forgiveness for placing his job before their marriage, and for the holidays and special occasions he missed just to meet a deadline at work. Tom was astounded when Susan revealed that she had also been on an inner journey. She was also looking for a new way of life, and for Susan that also involved changes in her lifestyle, work, and marriage as well. Both admitted that they still loved each other, but wanted more from marriage than just superficial affection and occasional nights out.

Tom and Susan sought out a minister known for her openness to spiritual seekers. Together, they made plans to face the cancer as a couple and begin a new life as partners, lovers, and friends. Their pastor taught them how to meditate and gave them spiritual affirmations for their health and relationship. Long evening walks along a nearby river and quiet weekends at their beach house replaced their once frantic schedule. They got to know each other all over again and began to like the persons they were becoming together. Tom confesses that it was like a second honeymoon: "I was falling in love all over again. I had forgotten how truly wonderful Susan was as a friend and partner." Susan echoes that sentiment, "For the first time in years, I could see the playful, loving friend who had been hiding for so long behind his computer, cell phone, and flip chart."

In his quest for physical healing, Tom began to consult a physician whose work united Western and complementary medicine. Every day, and especially during his chemotherapy treatments, Tom visualized healing light entering his body and gently flushing out his cancer cells. He imaged himself as healthy and whole in mind, body, and spirit. He saw God's love embodied in the healing light that filled his body.

Today, Tom is free of cancer. But more amazing to Tom, he and Susan have a beautiful baby. They have a chosen a new life as individuals and as a couple. They now each work half time in order to nurture their daughter and grow in the relationship as parents and lovers. Tom works at home as a consultant, alternating between advertising proposals and afternoons in the park with his daughter. Susan has learned to say no to evenings at the office and to insignificant projects that used to demand immediate attention. Susan and Tom have also chosen to reach out beyond their family. Tom volunteers as a communications advisor for a group of nonprofit organizations; Susan has found a greater sense of meaning as a hospice volunteer. Although they realize they are just beginners on the spiritual journey, Tom and Susan have become active in their congregation's centering prayer and young parents' groups.

Although Tom saw his cancer as a wake-up call, he doesn't believe that God caused his cancer. God simply invited him to choose life and become a new person in the midst of the spiritual and physical crisis. Tom affirms, "Now I am healthy and whole, because of the faith I found and the love that was given to me. Each day, I thank God for the wonder of my life, my beautiful wife and child, and the many opportunities I have to share the love I've been given. Ironically, without the threat of death, I would never have chosen life." In his own personal journey, Tom experienced a physical cure, but he also found a spiritual healing. Today, he feels whole in mind, body, spirit, and relationships. Now, he begins each day with the healing affirmation, "This is the day that [God] has made;/ Let us rejoice and be glad in it" (Ps. 118:24).

Encountering illness and death can transform our lives. When pain and illness shatter their usual sense of independence and invulnerability, many persons look at their lives and ask, "Is that all there is?" Moments of spiritual and emotional dislocation may awaken us to the surprises of grace that reveal there is always more to life than we can possibly imagine. Our initial disorientation may be the open door to a new orientation and a deeper relationship to the Spirit that moves within and beyond our lives. Beyond the bad news lies the good news that God is always there to show us the path toward healing and wholeness.

Such dislocating moments and times of threat can destroy us, but they can also transform us. Do you recall Leo Tolstoy's story *The Death of Ivan Illych?* Confronted by the reality of a life-threatening illness, Ivan—like Tom—cries out, "I want to live," but a voice within him whispers, "Do I want to live as I have before?" In moments of dislocation, we ask ourselves, "Do I really want to be made well? Do I really want something more out of life?" When we ask, "Is that all there is?" a still, small voice responds, "There is more to life than you can imagine, and when you say yes to Life, your life will be transformed and you will be healed!"

Sometimes the commitment to spiritual transformation becomes the catalyst for a lifestyle of healing that brings physical, emotional, and spiritual healing. Yet, you many not be cured. You may continue to live with a chronic illness or disability, but you still can be healed. You can experience wholeness and joy, whether you experience the world from the vantage point of a mountaintop or wheelchair. You can experience Shalom!

Something More

Before the voyages of Columbus and other European explorers, Western mapmakers erroneously sketched the words *ne plus ultra*, "there is no more," at the edges of their maps. After the voyages of Columbus and others, they revised their maps with the words *plus ultra*, "there is more," even though they could barely imagine the wonders of that mysterious western frontier.

The quest for something more has always been central to the spiritual journey. Whether or not we are aware of it, our lives are lived on many dimensions. Our bodies reveal Divine wisdom. Our thoughts and emotions reflect the handiwork of the Divine Artist. We are companions on a holy adventure in which each encounter or life situation invites us to journey toward uncharted frontiers of body, mind, and spirit. In each moment, we can bring healing to our world and contribute to the healing of the planet.

Today, one of the greatest frontiers of the human adventure involves the growing evidence that mind, body, and spirit exist in a dynamic synergy. As new scientific and medical worldviews emerge, we are challenged to revise our maps of reality and human life. But, we are also reminded that the deepest insights of the Jewish and Christian traditions provide the foundation for healing and wholeness in every life situation:

1. The heavens declare the glory of God, and so do our bodies.
2. God is working for healing and wholeness in all things.
3. We are children of God, endowed with the ability to creatively transform our lives and the world.
4. God's truth is present in all things; God is as fully present in the laboratory and operating room as in our houses of worship and moments of quiet prayer.
5. The quest for truth and healing in all its forms is a quest for the Divine.

Nowhere is this dynamic new vision of reality more visible than in the mysterious frontiers where faith and medicine meet. Ancient wisdom, contemporary science, and global spirituality are emerging as partners in the search for wholeness and healing. Grounded in the lively wisdom of the ages, a dynamic global spirituality is emerging that inspires and transforms the ancient wisdom of Judaism and Christianity.

The intricate connection of spirituality and health is nothing new in human history. In ancient societies as well as in early Judaism and Christianity, the role of healer, spiritual guide, and lawgiver were united in the religious leaders of the community. The religious activities of priests and shamans focused on integrating the order and harmony of the universe with the well-being of individuals and communities.

Issues of health and wholeness were essential to Hebraic spirituality. Healthy diet and behavior were grounded in the Divine Order of the universe and connected with faithfulness to God. Purity and cleanliness set the Hebrews apart from their neighbors and defined their unique relationship with God. *Shalom,* or dynamic wholeness, embraced the lifestyle of both persons and communities. Though it was seldom fully realized, the Divine order of the universe was reflected in the ordering of dinner table, ethics toward citizens and strangers, and justice toward the poor.

Many early Hebraic teachers believed that righteousness led to health and success, while sin issued in sickness and poverty. Although the book of Job challenged the linear connection between morality, success, and health, many later Jewish teachers—like today's wholistic health practitioners—still recognized that there was a significant, though not absolute, connection between mind, body, spirit, and relationships. Human life can be described in terms of a psychosomatic unity, in which the well-being of each part is related to the well-being of the whole. Physical well-being contributes to emotional and spiritual health. Emotional and spiritual health may also be a factor in physical and relational well-being.

The Hebrews believed that God created the world to be "very good," and that this goodness embraced physical existence, sexuality, family life, and vocation. God's wisdom is revealed in the heavens above and in the inner world of the cardiovascular, immune, and digestive systems. As Psalm 139 proclaims:

> For it was you who formed my inward parts;
>   you knit me together in my mother's womb.
> I praise you, for I am fearfully and wonderfully made.
>   (Ps. 139:13–14)

As children of the Divine Artist, we are "fearfully and wonderfully made." But so are all of God's creatures. In caring for our bodies and the bodies of others, we honor our Creator and bring healing to the world.

Although the early Hebrews were reluctant to consult local physicians because of their ties to the polytheism of the non-Jewish cultures that surrounded them, later Hebraic thought affirmed that medicine is a Divine gift to humankind. The book of Sirach, written two centuries before the time of Jesus of Nazareth, proclaims the Divine origins of medicine and affirms the creative relationship between spirituality and health, in which physicians, medicines, and prayers reflect the many manifestations of God's loving kindness.

> Honor physicians for their services,
>   for the [Eternal] created them;
> for their gift of healing comes from the Most High,
>   and they are rewarded by the king
> [God] created medicines out of the earth,
>   and the sensible will not despise them.
> Was not water made sweet with a tree
>   in order that its power might be known?
> And [God] gave skill to human beings
>   that God might be glorified in [the Divine's] marvel-
>   ous works.
> By them the physician heals and takes away pain;
>   the pharmacist makes a mixture from them.
> God's works will never be finished
>   and from [the Divine] health spreads over all the earth.
>
> My child, when you are ill, do not delay,
>   but pray to the [God who] will heal you.
> Give up your faults, and direct your hands rightly,
>   and cleanse your heart from sin
> Then give the physicians [their] place, for the Lord
>   created [them];
>   do not let [them] leave you, for you need [them.]
> There may come a time when your recovery lies in the

hands of physicians,
for they too pray to the Lord that God grant them
success in diagnosis
and healing for the sake of preserving life.
                              (Sir. 38:1–2, 4–10, 12–14)

Just a few centuries later, Christian theologians saw healing
and truth as a reflection of the universality of God's love and
guidance. They believed that wherever truth is found, God is
its source. In light of the growing interplay of spirituality and
medicine, we would also affirm that wherever healing is found,
whether in the operating room, the medical energy worker's
table, or the worship service, God is its source.

True to his Hebraic roots, Jesus of Nazareth, whose Hebrew
name "Yeshua" means "one who saves or makes whole," saw
spirituality as encompassing the whole person—body, mind,
spirit, and relationships. Jesus' response to illness reflected his
understanding of God's compassionate aim of abundant life
for all persons. While he recognized that the quality of our
spiritual lives and behavior may contribute both positively and
negatively to our health and well-being, Jesus did not blame
people for their diseases. Nor did Jesus see disease as a result of
Divine punishment for sinful behavior.

The presence of disease was an opportunity for compassion,
hospitality, and transformation, regardless of its origins. The
occurrence of illness also challenged people to place their trust
in the Divine Healer, whose love calls us to companionship
and creativity.

In the spirit of today's wholistic caregivers, Jesus utilized a
variety of approaches to heal people's diseases—faith and the
placebo effect, psychotherapeutic listening and confrontation,
healing touch and energy, healing at a distance, medicinal cures,
hospitality, and acceptance. Regardless of the medium of
healing, Jesus saw our relationship to God as central to the
healing process. Faithful prayer could move mountains and
bring healing to those who had been blind or paralyzed. Our

spiritual commitments connect us to an infinite supply of Divine energy, whose power can change our attitudes, open us to new possibilities, and transform even the cells of our bodies.

While Jesus' healings and those of his Hebraic predecessors are incomprehensible to those who see the world in terms of linear, mechanistic, cause-and-effect relationships, the new images of reality suggested by contemporary physics, environmental studies, chaos theory, and mind-body medicine reveal a vision of reality in which the interplay of spiritual commitment of persons and communities, a healthy social environment, and the subtle movements of God can bring new life to troubled bodies and minds. Although we do not expect the dead to rise or persons who are blind to recover their sight simply by the application of touch and saliva, Jesus' healing ministry and its Hebraic predecedents challenge us to embrace life's mysteries. Miraculous cures occur—for instance, at Lourdes, France, in healing services, or through the touch of a loving companion. We can neither control nor understand such healings, but we can open our minds to the Divine surprises hidden in the everyday.

Jesus' healings were grounded in his appreciation of the integrity and freedom of each person. While God seeks the healing of all persons, our attitudes, faith, and spiritual commitments may increase or decrease the flow of Divine energy into our lives. God does not force healing upon us, but gently invites us to embrace the healings and cures that arise from the Divine-human partnership.

In the spirit of his Hebraic ancestors, Jesus recognized the social dimensions of disease. With the Hebraic prophets, Jesus affirmed the relationship between social justice and health. Unhealthy economic and social structures lead to a greater incidence of disease in the community. In addition, Jesus recognized that disease isolated persons physically and socially. Then, as now, certain persons were ostracized because of their diseases. In contrast to the norms of his society, Jesus welcomed and touched persons whose diseases rendered them social and religious outcasts. Jesus' compassion inspired one physician to note that Jesus and Hippocrates are the twin founders of Western medicine.[1] Jesus and his Hebraic spiritual predecessors taught that when we face challenges of mind, body, and spirit, "there is more"—the Divine One is working in our lives to awaken us to the healing potential that is our birthright.

Healing the Body, Healing the Soul

The wall of separation that divided spirituality and medicine for nearly four centuries is crumbling. Medical scientists are rediscovering the wisdom of Jesus and the Hebraic prophets as well as the healing practices of other religious traditions and ethnic communities. They are learning that persons can change their lives and health outcomes through their spiritual commitments and religious practices.[2] Although medicine cannot fully encompass the Divine mystery incarnate in each person and in the ever-present and gentle movements toward healing, medical research has identified nine connections between spirituality, religious commitment, and overall health:

1. *Prayer, including intercessory prayer, can calm your spirit and promote physical healing for yourself and other persons.* Medical studies indicate that praying for another person, or intercessory prayer, promotes her or his recovery following heart bypass surgery. Persons who were part of groups whose members were the objects of prayer had quicker recoveries, with fewer side effects, than those who were part of the "control" group. Other studies indicate that prayer at a distance promotes the healing of wounds in mice and increases the rate of growth of fungi and grasses.

Physician Larry Dossey speaks of prayer as a nonlocal phenomenon that intimately connects us with persons across the street and across the planet. While scientists cannot verify the presence of God in their studies, many physicians, as well as persons of faith, believe that when we pray, we consciously connect with the Divine Wisdom that seeks wholeness for all things. We create a healing "field of force" around those for whom we pray. This Divine Wisdom is not just "out there," but is the deepest reality of all things. It is the heartbeat of love that pulses through every thought and emotion, bringing God's healing touch to every encounter. In praying for another, we become God's partners in seeking the other's well-being. As the stories of Jesus' healings indicate, our faith may enable Divine power to be intensified in certain situations.

No one can explain how prayer works and why it seems to change certain life situations. Along with certain physicians, scientists, and spiritual leaders, we believe that our prayers radiate across the universe, surrounding the objects of our prayer with positive energy. In the intricate web of relationships that characterizes the universe, described by both the new physics and biblical spirituality, our thoughts and prayers make a subtle difference in the well-being of others, even though they are seldom experienced at a conscious level by those for whom we pray. While prayer does not insure good health or prosperity, the simple practice of praying can improve your health and contribute to the well-being of others. As physician Larry Dossey aptly states, "Prayer is good medicine."

On this last point, we must raise a note of caution. In certain circles, persons are blamed for their illness or inability to get well. At virtually every talk we give, someone in the audience tells of a pious Christian or New Age teacher who has told them if they only had a more positive attitude, greater faith, or a larger prayer community, they or their loved ones would recover from illness. We affirm the power of faith and prayer to shape reality, but we also recognize a complex and dynamic ecology of health and healing. Prayer is just one factor among many in determining our physical and mental well-being. If prayer or spiritual maturity were the only factor in personal well being, then "saints" would always live to a ripe old age, while those who turn their backs on God and morality would die young. Further, we must also assert that the ultimate aim of prayer is not the promotion of physical well-being, but companionship with God and alignment with God's purposes for our lives and our planet.

When he was diagnosed with inoperable cancer, Bruce's friend Steve continued to commit himself to the spiritual practices and values he had lived by his whole life—daily prayer and meditation, service to the poor, regular worship. Steve recognized that God's power and his own faith are never measured by worldly success. "I will pray if it promotes a cure, but I will also pray even if there are no tangible changes in my physical condition."

Steve's name was listed on the "prayer lists" of churches throughout North America. Along with chemotherapy, Steve received the "laying of hands" from many friends and religious leaders, massage and energy work, and spiritual counsel. After a two-year pilgrimage with cancer, Steve succumbed. In his final days, Steve affirmed that his faith did not depend on finding a cure. "I wish that I had been cured of this cancer. But, I know that I have experienced a healing. I feel at peace. I know that God has been with me and that when I die, I will be in God's hands. God was with me in the cancer, and God will be with me in whatever comes next. I know that the prayers and imaging have made a difference. I did not expect a miracle, although I hoped for one. Perhaps I did receive a miracle—a greater awareness of the love of others and the love of God. For that I will always be grateful." Even in his final days, Steve continued to praise God for the wonder of life itself—sunset and dawn, the chirping of birds, and a loving spouse and friends. Although he might be described as a failure by those who see prayer as a way to control the uncontrollable or manipulate reality, Steve knew that his prayers were answered, for God was real in each moment's breath.

2. *Going to church or temple can improve your health.* Regular attendance at worship services has been identified as a factor in lower incidence of hypertension, heart disease, and cervical cancer. Positive relationships, grounded in the belief that life is

meaningful, that our actions and beliefs make a difference, and that God will provide for our deepest needs, translate into physical, emotional, and spiritual well-being.

People who participate in faith communities tend to live longer, have fewer incidents of serious illness, and cope better with life crises. As the biblical tradition states, "It is not good for a person to be alone" (Gen. 2:18 paraphrased). We are made for community. The sharing of joys and concerns in a safe environment connects us to the healing power of relationships. If, as some research indicates, loneliness can be a factor in heart disease, then, conversely, healthy relationships may be factors in overall well-being in mind, body, and spirit. We are happiest and healthiest when we have friends with whom we can share our joys and burdens. This sense of companionship and acceptance promotes well-being at the cellular and systemic levels.

Worship services and religious group activities provide a number of potentially health-affirming and calming activities: music, familiar rituals that root us in a larger reality than our own individual experience, a sense of community and group support, time out from everyday tensions and schedules, and friendship and socializing. For some persons, church or temple is the only place where they are touched in a healthy and supportive manner.

Barry and Ann Ulanov speak of spiritual experiences as awakening us to the "primal speech" of the universe. Familiar rituals, scriptures, and hymns enable us to experience the quieter, more peaceful time of childhood, even as they connect us at a primordial level with God's "still, small voice." According to physician Herbert Benson, remembering joyful worship experiences from childhood can nurture experiences of wholeness in the present moment:

> Even if you experience the ritual from an entirely
> different perspective of maturity, the words you read,
> the songs you sing, and the prayers you invoke will

soothe you in the same way that they did in what was perhaps a simpler time in your life…The brain retains a memory of the constellation of activities associated with the ritual, both the emotional content that allows the brain to weigh its importance and nerve cell firings, interactions, and chemical releases that were first activated.[3]

Worship brings us closer to God and to our neighbors. While science cannot prove the existence of God, the simple recognition that we are not alone in the universe, and that there is a Holy Reality who seeks our well-being and invites us to be partners in healing our lives and mending the world, makes our problems smaller and our resources larger. Participation in a worshiping community provides countless opportunities for support, spiritual guidance, and encouragement in times of crisis, such as illness and bereavement, as well as for selfless service to the larger community. Virtually every active participant in a religious community can testify to the outpouring of care and support he or she has received when ordinary life was shattered by accident, disease, or death.

When Ann's father, George, suffered a paralyzing stroke, the women of the church came to her rescue. Ann found it difficult to visit her father because of her lifelong disabilities. Recognizing her need, the women's guild provided Ann with regular transportation, took her to lunch and movies, and insured that the nursing staff at the convalescent hospital recognized their interest in George's condition. Following her father's death two years later, Ann recounts, "I couldn't have made it without the church. I know God exists now. I saw God in the faces of the people driving me to the nursing home, bringing me lunch and taking me to a movie, doing yard work, and making sure that the nurses were aware of any problems my father had." Deborah, one of the guild members, simply states, "This is what it means to follow God—to reach out to persons in need. I know that had I been in Ann's situation, my church would have been there for me, too! Faith is not just about what God does for me, but what I can do to bring beauty and joy to the lives of others. This is my gift back to God."

In the life of healthy religious communities, there is an interplay of giving and receiving. We attend church and temple not merely to experience peace of mind and better health, but to serve God through acts of praise and care for our immediate neighbors and for our planet. Purely self-serving faith isolates us from God and our neighbors, while service connects us with the movements of healing that flow through all things. Authentic worship enlarges our personal stature in such a way that we identify the well-being of others with our own well-being. We find our greatest happiness in bringing beauty to the world, regardless of whether our health improves.

Simon confesses that he returned to Friday night services at first for social reasons. The temple had a singles group, and he wanted to make new friends and perhaps find a life partner. Although he enjoyed the social life, he fell in love with the Hebrew melodies and sense of God's presence and power in the world. The traditional Hebraic praises became his spiritual mantras throughout the week. But, more than that, he came to realize that worship is completed by acts of kindness and justice. Simon did find a life partner at the temple, but also discovered a world in need of healing and his own unique role in mending the earth. Simon's experience of "remembered wellness" went far beyond his own personal spirituality, and led him to promote that same well-being among those who have been forgotten by our success-oriented culture.

3. *Meditative practices such as centering prayer and the relaxation response calm the mind and bring about short and long-term health benefits, including lowering blood pressure, enhancing immune system functioning, and decreasing the heart rate.*

Herbert Benson, who pioneered the scientific studies of meditative practices, believes that meditation is an antidote for the "fight-or-flight response," which is epidemic in our fast-paced, frenetic, and competitive society. The calm of body and mind elicited by meditation and focused prayer gives us a mini-Sabbath, a time of rest and recreation, in the midst of a demanding work week.

Health involves an appropriate balance of work and play, and activity and quiet. As American culture only too graphically demonstrates, people are made for activity. But as the image of the Sabbath and the prayer life of Jesus suggest, we are also made for quiet receptivity. Meditation breaks the pattern of constantly swirling thoughts and allows us to experience the deep stillness that brings peace and focus to our lives. In entering the spacious realm of Divinity, we experience the "relaxation response," which transforms our experience of time from scarcity to abundance. We discover that we have more time than we had imagined when we operate from the Divine stillness. Answers to problems come more easily. We experience less panic and stress when unexpected problems surface. In the intricate interplay of mind and body, when the mind is at peace, the body also finds rest.

Meditation is a significant factor in breaking down the cycle of stress and distress. Physicians note that the majority of patient visits are related to people's inability to deal creatively with the stresses of life. Medical studies cite a clear link between chronic stress and familiar complaints such as headaches, backaches, muscle tension, insomnia, and stomach problems. High blood pressure, heart disease, ulcers, asthma, and eczema can be exacerbated by emotional stress. Stress has even been identified as a factor in hormonal imbalances that interfere with the healthy functioning of the reproductive system.

The constant wear and tear of stress also depresses the immune system and makes us more vulnerable to colds and flu. In one study, researchers found that persons who experienced severe, chronic (lasting one month or more), stressful life events, such as unemployment, underemployment, or interpersonal difficulties, were between two to three times more likely to develop colds than those without such experiences.

Stress is inevitable in life. But, how we deal with stress may be a matter of life and death. Quiet moments of meditation and the expansive vision of worship prevent stress from becoming distress and enable us to deal creatively with the challenges of life.

Even religious professionals can succumb to stress-related illness. The rabbi of a growing congregation, Sol, was near burnout. His days seemed to have no end as he ran from meeting to meeting and service to service. He seldom found time for himself or his family. He no longer had time to study and began to see his sermons as a chore rather than a blessing. After days of waking up fatigued and feeling anxious throughout the day, Sol decided to take action. He made an appointment with his physician, who confirmed a relationship between the breakneck pace of his life and his overall health. His doctor prescribed medication for his mild hypertension, but also advised Sol to embark on a regimen of exercise, healthy diet, and meditation. Sol began to meditate twenty minutes every morning and evening. At first, he couldn't imagine how he could find enough time to meditate amid his busy schedule. But, he persevered, despite his doubts. The results were dramatic—he no longer felt as anxious and stressed-out by the events of the day; his blood pressure lowered, although he still continued to take a maintenance dose of medication for high blood pressure—and he began to discern the important and the unimportant in his professional life. Sol notes that meditation, along with study, has become the mainstay of his daily life. "As odd as it may seem," Sol admits, "since I began to meditate forty minutes each day, I have more time and energy for my family and my work. I feel better and no longer worry about finishing every task. Meditation has helped me to trust God's care for my life and my congregation. I love preaching again, and am gratified by the positive responses I am receiving from my congregation."

4. *Active, vivid imagination can save your life and improve your health.* Radiation oncologist O. Carl Simonton and therapist Stephanie Matthews Simonton believe that a healthy imagination is essential to improving the quality of emotional and physical well-being of persons with cancer.[4] They affirm that inability to imagine a positive future or options for change depresses the immune system, and increases our vulnerability to illness. Conversely, visualization exercises open patients to new possibilities for change and empower them to respond creatively to the diagnosis of cancer and other serious illnesses. Visions of hope and empowerment may activate the immune system in its response to cancer and other diseases. Accordingly, many medical professionals teach their patients to visualize healing light surrounding, neutralizing, and flushing out the cancer cells from their body.

While the research on the positive benefits of imagery and visualization is still at the infancy stage, many persons claim to experience greater well-being through secular and religious forms of positive imagery. For example, during her chemotherapy treatments, Rebecca imagines God's healing light infusing her whole being along with the medication. She affirms, "Visualizing a healing light calms me down, but it also gives me a sense of empowerment—I can do something to support my own healing process. I am not a victim of cancer or a passive recipient of medical care." In assessing her medical condition Rebecca confesses, "I don't know if the imagery destroys the cancer cells or activates the chemotherapy. But, I know for a fact that I feel better and stronger, and am no longer nervous about chemotherapy and its side effects."

5. *Hope can open the door to new possibilities for health and wellness.* Martin Seligman, the author of *Learned Optimism,* sees clear physiological and psychological benefits to optimism.[5] Hope and hopelessness can cure or kill. According to Seligman, negative thinkers have weaker immune systems, succumb more often to infectious diseases, and, after the age of forty-five, face more major health problems than optimistic persons. Other

researchers have concluded that feelings of hopelessness and despair can contribute to problems in the immune and cardiovascular systems.

In the intricate relationship of mind and body, faith can transform physiology. Hope awakens us to an open future in which change and growth are always possibilities. In so doing, we open the door to novelty, empowerment, and adventure. When we are optimistic about the future, our immune system says yes to life.

Hope was at the heart of Julia's personal transformation. Stuck in a job she hated, Julia lived for the weekends. But, the weekends were no better than her long, pointless days at the office. Wearied by the previous week's tasks and her own negative attitudes, Julia spent most of the weekend sleeping, watching old movies on cable TV, and eating junk food. She complained about being lonely, but seldom reached out to her friends. When Monday came around again, she felt as if she had wasted one more week of her life.

Julia's life and health continued to deteriorate until a friend's challenge changed everything. "Julia, you're killing yourself. You go from day to day like a zombie. Don't you want to live—and greet each day with a smile?" As she pondered her friend's comments, Julia wondered if she could truly change. She even wondered if she really wanted to change. After all, if she quit complaining, she would have to find a new script and a new way of relating to others. Realistically, Julia realized that the process of personal change would take time. Yet the first step, the realization that today could be different from yesterday, was the image of hope Julia needed. Step by step, she opened herself to new possibilities: She began to see a therapist who challenged her to embrace new attitudes and behaviors; she joined a gym and began a modest exercise program; she went hiking or visited friends rather than watching TV on the weekends. Julia began to read spiritual literature and eventually joined a young adults' group at church. She even to began to volunteer as a tutor at a local elementary school.

Once she recognized that she could change in small parts of her life, a whole new world opened up for her. Julia is now vital and energetic. She has found a more fulfilling job, and she is active in service programs related to her church. Julia admits that the process of change is not always easy, and that sometimes she falls back into old habits, but "once I realized I could change, I had hope that I would change. Now, I believe that I can make a difference wherever I am. The person I am now amazes me." Although Julia spends more Sunday mornings in hiking than in church, she admits that God has been part of her new life. "God was always in my life. But, until I opened the door, God couldn't enter. God had a whole world of possibilities waiting for me, and I didn't know it. Now each day is an adventure. My life may be ordinary to others, but to me, there is a surprise around every corner."

6. *Reaching out to others can promote physical and emotional well-being.* In *The Healing Power of Doing Good,* Allan Luks asserts that people who help others report better health than their peers.[6] The release of endorphins that occurs when people reach out in service not only relieves pain but also stimulates the pleasurable feelings described as "the helper's high." Volunteers claim both long-term and short-term emotional benefits, including a greater sense of calm and relaxation, self esteem, and optimism. One study notes that simply watching a video of Mother Teresa serving the poor in Calcutta's slums enhances the antibodies necessary for fighting colds and infections. Of course, authentic wholeness involves really helping others and not just thinking about it!

Love and care are not governed by the bottom line. The spiritual wisdom of Judaism and Christianity tells us that the more you give, the happier you are. As we support the healing of others, we experience greater energy and wellness. As the biblical tradition affirms, giving and receiving are united in promoting the well-being of everyone, including yourself. In your love and care for others, you awaken to a relational revolution in which the resources of the universe flow through your life to enrich everyone you meet.

Biblical wisdom calls us to love our neighbors as ourselves, and even extend our love to the stranger and the enemy. As Jesus notes, our care for the "least of these" is our gift to God. Loving service releases us from the burden of self-preoccupation and connects us with the dynamic of companionship with God and the world.

7. *The right kind of touch can heal your life.* We are created to be touched in a loving manner. Jesus and the Jewish healers who preceded him healed persons by touch. Studies indicate that infants cannot flourish without loving touch. In today's pediatric intensive care units, volunteers caress, hold, and give healing touch to premature babies. Adults cannot live without healthy touch either. Loving touch, especially of social outcasts, was central in Jesus' healing ministry. The skin is the largest organ of our bodies and it is meant to receive the nurture of gentle affirmation and affection. Without loving touch, our bodies and spirits wither. One form of healing touch, therapeutic touch, has been found to lower blood pressure, enhance immune system functioning, and encourage feelings of peace and wholeness. Others have found greater wholeness through Reiki healing touch, massage, shiatsu, and other forms of healing energy. Today, most major airports have centers where tired and anxious travelers can receive "seated massage" as a way of connecting with the wellsprings of health and vitality. The Divine energy of the universe flows through our fingers to transform the bodies, minds, and spirits of others. Reaching out in love, we experience God's touch in the hands of a friend or a spouse.

Bruce has found healing touch to be an important part of his marriage and parenting. On almost a daily basis, he gives a brief massage or energy treatment to his wife Kate and their son Matt. These healing touches have bonded them as a family and have reminded them that wholeness and service are at the heart of their relationship as a family. Married to a professional massage therapist and energy worker, Bruce receives as much as he gives in the circle of healing that connects his family. Healthy touch is a way of life that constantly reminds us that there is always something we can do to support the well-being of our families and friends.

Members of the church where Kate is the senior pastor often ask for a brief massage or Reiki treatment following worship services. Committed to the highest standards of professional conduct and care, Kate has found healing touch to be an important complement to her leadership as a pastor and spiritual guide.

8. *Moving with the Spirit.* We are made for movement. Our body is the "temple of God" and by moving with the Spirit, we attune ourselves to God's dynamic movements within our lives. We are meant for action, not stagnation. The yin and yang of meditation and action complement one another in the process of healing and wholeness. Even a modest, non-aerobic exercise can improve your overall physical, emotional, and spiritual health.

Today, many persons are "prayer walkers" who join aerobic exercise with spiritual centering. As they take their daily walk, they open themselves to a higher creativity through meditative prayer, affirmations, or prayers of thanksgiving and intercession. In moving our bodies, we awaken our minds to the rhythm of a dancing God.

Prayer walking is at the heart of Michael's spiritual life. Each morning at sunrise, Michael fast-walks through his suburban neighborhood, repeating to himself a holy word from the Jewish mystical tradition. Although he is constant movement, Michael feels centered and at peace. In the last few minutes of his walk, Michael visualizes his friends and family, surrounding them with the light of God's creation and seeing God's light bursting forth from their lives.

9. *Soul food and spiritual growth.* The Jewish and Christian traditions both affirm the relationship between our diet and our spiritual lives. Hebraic law asserted that our relationship

with the Holy One is connected with the food we eat and the just distribution of economic resources. Today, researchers confirm that the dietary rules of the Hebraic tradition promote physical well-being and longevity. Orthodox Jews, along with Seventh Day Adventists and Latter Day Saints (Mormons), enjoy longer life spans and better overall health as a result of their commitment to a biblically based diet and affirmation of family life.

While the Christian tradition has no specific dietary guidelines, Jesus' followers spoke of the body as "the temple of God." We are called to glorify God in our bodies by our personal lifestyle, commitment to making adequate food available to all persons, and healthy eating habits (1 Cor. 6:12–20).

The table fellowship at Passover and the celebration of communion remind us that our diet has ethical implications. We cannot claim to follow a spiritual path if we neglect the hungry or live in a manner that destroys the environment or promotes economic injustice. Our diet expresses our connectedness with the whole earth as well as the affirmation of our own well-being. While no one diet fits all persons, diets low in fat and high in vegetables and fruits join physical health with social conscience.

The image of Shalom is a constant reminder that mind, body, spirit, and relationships are intimately connected. We are meant for health and wholeness. Although disease and death are part of reality, we can choose to claim God's abundant life by committing ourselves to a lifestyle that embraces spiritual growth, physical exercise, healing imagination, and sound dietary principles.

Spiritual Growth in Hard Times

But there is more to the healing power of faith than just prevention. The faith that promotes overall well-being also makes a difference during times of illness. Scientists note that our spiritual commitments not only promote good health but also enable us to respond more creatively to sickness and bereavement.[7] Committed to a healthy relationship with God and our neighbors, we have all the resources we need to find peace of mind as well as physical and relational well-being even in difficult situations.

1. *Religiously active persons recover more quickly from surgery.* In one study of people with heart disease, involving 232 patients over the age of fifty-five who had open heart surgery, those whose faith inspired strength, comfort, and solace were three times more likely to survive than those who did not have such a faith.[8]

Our religious faith and spiritual commitments place illness in a larger perspective and remind us that we can find meaning in life's challenges. While God does not punish us with illness or give us illness as a means of strengthening our character, we believe that God's presence in our lives provides opportunities for growth in otherwise difficult situations. We can experience greater personal stature by placing our suffering and vulnerability in God's care and enabling God to inspire us to greater hope and compassion. Although God's care embraces all persons, trust in God awakens us to greater personal hope and strength. With the apostle Paul, we can affirm that "in all things God works for the good of those who love [God]" (Rom. 8:28, NIV).

Andrea's recovery from heart surgery was a difficult one. At times, she felt that the cure was worse than the ailment, especially as she battled an ongoing infection that left her bedridden for weeks. "What got me through," Andrea admits, "was the faith of friends that bolstered my own faith. On my lowest days, when I felt like giving up, their kind words and prayers sustained my spirit, until I could believe once more. I made it through because I knew that God was with me and God still had work to do in my life."

2. *Religiously active people cope better with chronic health conditions.* Faith enables us to cope with life's challenges with greater peace of mind. Prayer, meditation, and religious activity

benefit persons whose illnesses have psychological and stress-related components, as well as those whose illnesses are physically based. Belief in the goodness of the universe and companionship with God enables us to transcend our current physical condition and discover the surprising healing resources of body, mind, and spirit. Inspired by the presence of God and the support of others, we become agents of our own healing, rather than victims of powers entirely beyond our control.

Herbert Benson states that we are "wired for God." While science cannot speculate about the role of God in health and healing or quantify the relationship between spiritual practices and Divine activity, we believe that a gentle and unceasing movement toward wholeness exists in every cell and organ of our bodies. Religious activities, such as prayer, meditation, and worship, open us to greater infusions of healing energy and enable us to marshal the resources we need to experience wholeness even when we face chronic and life-threatening illness. Benson describes this inherent mental and physical wellness as "remembered wellness."[9] God is at work in our lives, giving us strength and hope when life seems most difficult. Spiritual activities enable body as well as mind to "remember" at the deepest level the unseen, but constantly working, power of God's healing touch.

Following a recent surgery, Bruce's wife Kate experienced postoperative complications that meant a return to the hospital for further tests and procedures. On the eve of one of the tests, Kate had to take a medication whose side effects are particularly unpleasant. She was frightened and anxious at the prospect of taking this medication once again. She knew that she would have a sleepless and unpleasant night. But, she found comfort and peace as she said a spiritual affirmation with each sip, "With God's help, I can do this…with God's help I can do this…with God's help, I can do this." Kate could take her medication in a holy way because she recognized that her pain was not the only reality, but part of a larger matrix, which included her own spiritual centeredness and God's healing presence. She knew that God was with her, and together they would make it through the night.

3. Studies indicate that hospital rooms that provide open and attractive vistas stimulate the recovery process. Our physical environment can promote either hope or hopelessness. Unbounded vistas inspire us to envisage our own unique possibilities for growth and change. They remind us that with God as our companion, there are no dead ends. God makes a way where there is no way!

Today, world-renowned medical centers, such as the Georgetown University Medical Center, have planted gardens in order to nurture the bodies and spirits of patients, visitors, and medical staff. The experience of beauty and expansive horizons promotes hope and happiness, and activates the body's inherent healing processes.

God gave us the beauty of the color purple, the Grand Canyon, the Pacific Ocean, and the human face. God implanted an urge toward beauty in each one of us, which is nourishment for our souls. While noise and sight pollution may be as harmful as air pollution, beauty and spacious horizons inspire hope and courage when we face the daily challenges of chronic and life-threatening illness.

The studies cited in this chapter are just a small part of the emerging synergy of spirituality and medicine. Secular scientists are discovering the healing power residing in the interplay of ancient wisdom, contemporary science, and global spirituality in the process of healing. When we commit ourselves to personal and relational transformation in the context of healthy communities and spiritual practices, the whole universe supports our quest for wholeness of body, mind, and spirit. We can improve our health and deal creatively with chronic and life-threatening ailments. Although the problems of life may not go away, we can still find healing and new life.

CHAPTER THREE

Prescriptions for Wholeness

The medical evidence is clear. Our beliefs and religious practices promote wellness and stimulate recovery from illness. To persons of faith, the scientific research reflects a deeper metaphysical reality. While the existence of this deeper spiritual reality cannot be measured fully in terms of the scientific studies whose purpose is to assess the relationship of religious behaviors and physiological outcomes, persons of faith affirm that the Divine Spirit aims at wholeness in all things. This ever-present Spirit, or *Shekinah*, is the indwelling energy of balance, order, and healing in every cell in our bodies and in our lives as a totality. When we are attuned to this spiritual energy, we can experience greater health and well-being as well as peace and serenity in difficult situations.

The challenge for most people is to discover ways in which they can be open to this energy in their everyday lives both to promote good health and respond to illness. Today, we have the unique opportunity to employ the insights of the emerging partnership of faith and science in our quest for physical, spiritual, and emotional well-being. Because mind, body, and spirit seamlessly interpenetrate one another, spiritual practices nurture well-being and reduce pain, while physical activity stimulates creativity and balance in mind and spirit. Jesus' healing ministry reminds us that well-being emerges from many sources and techniques. While each person uniquely embodies the Divine quest for Shalom, or wholeness, certain tools for transformation energize body, mind, and spirit to bring wholeness to ourselves and others. We caught a glimpse of these tools for personal transformation in chapter 2. In this chapter, we will show you how to use these tools to promote wholeness and respond to sickness. In so doing, we are following a time-honored practice that joins theological reflection and spiritual guidance by (1) presenting a vision of reality in which God is the ever-present force of healing and wholeness in life (chapters 1, 2, and 5); (2) affirming that we can experience God's healing and empowering presence in our personal and communal lives (chapter 2); (3) providing a flexible path by which we can experience the healing and wholeness in our lives (chapters 3 and 4). In this and the next chapter, we will show you how to embody the wisdom found in the growing interplay of spirituality and medicine.

While the primary orientation of this book is health rather than pathology, we recognize that for many persons, the quest for wholeness begins with the "wake-up call" of chest pains, obesity, a lump, or general anxiety and discomfort. Although we will look at these as spiritual tools in the context of responding to illness, it is clear that any practice that brings greater wholeness and comfort when we are ill equally supports our well-being when we are healthy. In the healing ecology of life, we recognize that when we seek our own wholeness, we contribute to the healing of the world. We also enable God to be more active in healing ourselves and others. As the wisdom of the Kabbalah affirms, "The impulse below calls for an impulse from above." We become God's partners in *tikkun olam*, "mending the world" one moment at a time.

Transformed Minds, Transformed Bodies

A student once asked the Kotziker Rebbe, "Where is God?" The Rebbe replied, "Wherever you let God in." Spiritual practices enable us to let God's healing energy into our lives—and those of people for whom we care—in order to heal, transform, and comfort.

Judaism and Christianity affirm that we are always free to choose health and wholeness in difficult times. While we cannot always change the events in our lives or our overall health condition, we can choose a spiritual response to every challenge and crisis we face. A transformed mind can ease your pain and suffering, and improve our overall well-being. Changing the way we look at ourselves and the world may even transform the cells of our bodies.

Five spiritual attitudes promote wholeness and support the healing process—the wholeness of mind, body, and spirit— whether or not we are physically cured.

First, *don't blame yourself!* When she was diagnosed with ovarian cancer, Diane's first thought was, "Now, I'm finally being punished for my sixties lifestyle. If I'd chosen chastity rather than the summer of love, I wouldn't have cancer now!" Despite her self-blame, Diane found both a good medical team and a supportive spiritual coach who reminded her that morality and longevity do not always coincide; saints die in their youth and murderers live into old age with never a sick day.

Like Diane, we all look for a reason for sickness and death. Some simply say, "It's God's mysterious plan," while others assert that illness must be the result of Divine punishment for our sins, or an inexorable cosmic karma that follows us from life to life. Many traditional Christians and Jews believe that there is a one-to-one correspondence between our spiritual lives and our personal prosperity and health condition. When things go wrong, they assume they didn't pray enough or violated some spiritual law. After all, it's often easier for most of us to blame ourselves rather than God, our families, or society.

Other spiritual seekers suffer from what has recently been described as "New Age guilt." They believe that positive attitudes, meditation, exercise, affirmations, and a healthy diet guarantee a happy, healthy, and successful life. When illness strikes mind or body, they assume their personal negativity must be responsible for their condition. They assume that the universe is punishing them for not perfectly following the directions for health and prosperity. Yet, excessive guilt creates a circle of pain and impotence, which, according to some medical research, may even depress the immune system.

Although this book is grounded in the belief that persons' attitudes, behaviors, and spiritual commitments do play a role in their health and illness, we see health and illness as the result of many factors—including genetics and environment, family of origin and lifestyle, attitudes and nutrition, spiritual commitment and chance. In life, some things are simply out of our control, despite our best moral and spiritual efforts.[1]

While some people marvel at the healings of Jesus and certain Hebraic spiritual leaders, we must remind you that each person who received a cure from the hand of Jesus or his Hebraic predecessors eventually died. Even the healthiest lifestyle and most committed faith cannot immunize us from aging, accident, and death. Our choices make a difference, but we are not omnipotent. When illness strikes, we need to let go of the "blame game" and remember the wisdom of Viktor Frankl, who noted that although we cannot absolutely control our environment, health condition, or the political realities that shape our lives, we can, moment by moment, choose our attitude toward the unwanted moments of life. Our choice for freedom and health reflects God's choice for health and prosperity in our lives. God wants each one of us, and all persons, to have abundant life, and is working in every event to support our aim at authentic wholeness.

Jesus of Nazareth was once asked why a man was born blind (Jn. 9:1–7). His disciples wondered if the man's blindness was due to his sins or his parents' moral improprieties. Although Jesus denied that the man's illness was the result of his own sinful behavior, either in this lifetime or before he was born, or the prenatal sins of his parents, Jesus refused to give a clear answer to their academic question. In the spirit of the Hebraic prophets, he responded to pain wherever he found it. After he prayerfully applied a mud poultice on the blind man's eyes, Jesus commanded him to wash his eyes in the nearest pool. Rather than spending endless hours in theological analysis or personal blame, Jesus responded compassionately to the man's need. He reminded his followers then and now that our primary obligation is to bring healing and comfort to the sick while we are able to, even if their behavior has been a contributing factor in their illness.

In the intricate web of relationships, sometimes there is *no one specific* cause of health and illness. But, whatever our condition and however the illness came about, we can choose to nurture healing thoughts when we let go of inappropriate guilt and access the life-promoting practices of forgiveness and compassion for ourselves and others. The wisdom of the "Serenity Prayer" reminds us to be as gentle to ourselves as we would be to others in terms of what is beyond our control, even as we take responsibility for what is obviously in our control.

Second, **take on more responsibility**. This is the other side of the "Serenity Prayer." When we let go of what is not in our power, we can realistically change those things that are in our power. In the ecology of life, we are neither impotent nor omnipotent, and this realization can make all the difference in the world as we seek to bring healing to our lives.

Judaism and Christianity are practical religions. Within the context of the limitations placed upon us by our past, our environment, and our mortality, we are called to be God's partners in healing our lives and mending the world.

Tom's spiritual transformation (in chapter 2) came when he truly heard Jesus' question, "Do you want to be made well?" and knew that his response was a matter of spiritual and physical life and death. When Tom said "yes" to Jesus' question, he claimed the ever-present Divine power that enabled him to change his life. Ironically, the other side of letting go of guilt is claiming our power to transform ourselves and the world.

Each year at Yom Kippur, worshipers affirm that regardless of the past, we can change our lives for the better. With God's help, we can always do something to turn our lives around and begin, however modestly, a new path toward healing of mind, body, spirit, and relationships. In honestly facing our imperfections, habitual behaviors, and the pain we have caused others, we can make a new beginning not only during the High Holy Days but also with each new day.

Illness often encourages passivity. In our pain and vulnerability, we are tempted to act as if we are helpless and foolish children, surrendering our power to spouses, significant others, and physicians. To a man who had been a passive victim for nearly forty years, Jesus commanded, "Stand up," and he walked forward to a new life (Jn. 5:1–9). Our recovery often depends on choosing to stand on our own two feet. Although every healing path has its built-in risks, if we are not committed to our own healing process, who will be?

Western technological medicine frequently encourages passivity. Hospitals nurture uniformity through the "stripping process." Upon entry into today's temples of technology, many of us—like prisoners of war—relinquish our power to choose the course of our treatment and our future well-being as we surrender our clothing and medications to medical professionals. Yet, the vision of healing and wholeness we advocate in this book invites us to become partners with God and our physicians. We are not helpless children, despite the severity of our diagnosis. As long as we are able, we should take the same responsibility for our health as we do for our finances, children's education, and family vacations. In the hospital setting, we can work with medical professionals by letting them know what we need in order to facilitate the healing process. We can bring pictures, CD's, videos, and books to bolster our spirits and nurture our spiritual center. We can explore complementary as well as technological forms of health care. We can ask for a room with a view, and if we cannot get a room with a view, we can create a place of beauty by bringing flowers and pictures into the most sterile ward.

From the very beginning of your medical relationship, you need to meet your physician and other health care givers as equal partners in the healing process. This means claiming appropriate responsibility for every aspect of your medical situation, including gathering data, exploring complementary approaches, and following appropriate doctor's orders. Bernie Siegel, the noted oncologist and author of *Love, Medicine, and Miracles* (New York: Harper Row, 1986), affirms that the interplay of commitment to spiritual transformation, personal empowerment, and openness to the Divine characterizes what he describes as "exceptional cancer patients." These exceptional patients trust their own judgment and take responsibility for their decisions because they have cultivated a sense of confidence in their inner resources and in Divine guidance. They respect their physicians and honor their guidance, but also recognize that "M.D." is not the abbreviation for "medical deity." They ask questions, challenge unnecessary or debilitating medical treatments, and explore options. They realize that their health is too important to leave in the hands of "experts." They see their bodies as "temples of God," regardless of their physical condition, and they aim to treat them in a holy manner.

By taking responsibility for their well-being, they may even become their physicians' teachers as they gather information off the internet, describe their responses to specific medications or complementary health remedies, and share their spiritual insights. Finally, as empowered reflections of Divine creativity, they refuse to accept the limitations others may place upon them. Their own affirmative spirituality is an antidote to the "medical hexing," and negative prognoses that often go on in medical contexts. The exceptional patients realize the statistical nature of medical diagnoses and the realities of their illnesses. But, they do not conform to the limits, side effects, and life expectancies that physicians and other health care professionals may place upon them. Exceptional patients know that in the interplay of Divine inspiration and human creativity, surprising events may occur—life may triumph over death.

When Seth was diagnosed with an illness that statistically predicted death within five years for ninety percent of those diagnosed, he was initially overwhelmed with fear. "I'll never make it to forty," he said to himself. After the initial shock wore off, Seth experienced a personal epiphany at the Rosh Hashanah (New Year's) service at the temple. As the new year was hailed by blasts of the shofar, he realized that he could also make a new beginning. He realized that the dire statistics relating to his illness described the fate of persons in general and no particular person such as himself. While he recognized that his illness could kill him, Seth discovered a truth that meant the difference between spiritual life and death as it related to his own life. "Yes, the chances are only ten percent that persons like myself will survive five years. But, I aim to be one of the ten percent. If this were the lottery, I would consider myself a lucky man!" Seven years later, Seth is free of symptoms. His journey toward wholeness was demanding and difficult. It involved a marriage of the most sophisticated medical technologies, wholistic health practices, and spiritual resources. He attributes his recovery to his renewed faith and spiritual practice following the New Year's epiphany. "I know that God is with me, and that even if I die, God will be with me."

Today, a growing number of persons refuse to see the diagnosis of AIDS or HIV as a death sentence. Buoyed by advances in medicine and the examples of those who have chosen to be agents rather than victims in facing AIDS and HIV, they choose life daily through meditation, healing imagery, self-forgiveness, exercise, and participation in experimental and commonplace medical procedures. Reaching out to others, they find comfort in prayer, massage, Reiki healing touch, and therapeutic touch. They remain connected to God and to life, regardless of what the future brings.

Even persons with serious mental illnesses can claim a level of creative responsibility for their lives. Before his father's paralyzing strokes, Bruce's brother Bill had never lived alone, paid bills, or taken care of his car. Because of this brother's diagnosis with a schizo-affective disorder, Bruce worried that his brother would not make it on his own. But, with the support of friends from the church and Bruce's coaching, Bill has become self-reliant. While his life is not easy, Bill has created a life for himself both during his father's illness and following his father's death. He couldn't do it alone, but with the care of friends, family, and the church, he discovered courage and talent that he had not previously imagined. Like Bill, we are all stronger and more creative than we imagine. We can face our deepest fears and conquer them with the companionship of God and others. Our small steps toward self-responsibility often lead to great achievements in self-discovery!

Third, *cultivate a positive and hopeful attitude toward life.* Illness often constricts the boundaries of our lives. The once-spacious world of endless possibility shrinks to the limits of our hospital room and medical diagnosis. While seconds stretch to infinity, the future is often dominated by the pain of the present moment and fear of future discomfort. Hopelessness confines us to the prison of the present moment. Authentic hope opens us to surprising possibilities hidden in even the most difficult situations. As scientific research on the placebo and nocebo effects suggests, our beliefs may be embodied in the form of positive and negative physical symptoms.

Hope is not a matter of wishful thinking, but is a spiritual virtue grounded in the interplay between personal freedom and Divine possibility. As we noted in chapter 2, hope is the gift of an open future that arises from God's ever-present creativity. Hope is the exodus that brings us out of oppression in Egypt and gives us the vision of a new future in the promised land. Hope shows us that beyond the crucifixion, there is an Easter Sunday and the triumph of life over the forces of death and destruction. When we recognize that we live in an open system in which surprise, novelty, and synchronicity constantly bring forth new possibilities, we can say yes to life in all its pain and complexity.

In a time of personal and national upheaval, the prophet Jeremiah heard God's promise for himself and his people: "For surely I know the plans I have for you, says the LORD, plans for your welfare and not for harm, to give you a future with hope" (Jer. 29:11).

As the exiles in Babylon heard these words, they knew that their future was in the hands of a loving and empowering God. The Babylonian oppressor could not ultimately define their reality. Their oppression was real, and they had to acknowledge their homesickness and despair, but beneath the pain was God's irresistible vision of a hopeful and abundant future. Poverty, depression, HIV/AIDS, and cancer can all appear to block the path to the future; but none of them can destroy the life-giving hope that comes from a relationship with the Source of Love and Possibility.

A hopeful attitude opens the door to the Divine energy and healing power that transform both mind and body. In contrast, hopelessness and despair may weaken the cardiovascular and immune systems. Studies indicate that persons who suffer heart attacks while depressed (or become severely depressed following a heart attack) are more likely to die in the following six to twenty-four months than those who are optimistic and hopeful about their lives.[2]

Although it takes great resolve to focus on the positive when life has you down, remember that the best view for seeing stars is often found when you are lying on your back. Authentic realism embraces hope and fear, surprise and statistics, in its twin affirmation of life's beauty, goodness, and possibility as well as life's pain and injustice.

Hope is connected with a sense of humor that may be the difference between life and death. For Norman Cousins, laughter was truly the best medicine.[3] Diagnosed with a rare and debilitating illness, Cousins experienced the healing power of hope and self-transcendence through humor. Confined to a hospital bed, Cousins viewed taped episodes of "Candid Camera" and Marx brothers' movies. He laughed so hard that members of the medical staff suggested that he leave the hospital in order not to disturb the other patients. And he did not return!

In his reflections on his recovery, Cousins noted that laughter rejuvenates the body and mind. It also relaxes the muscles, reduces blood pressure and heart rate, and reduces nervous tension. Cousins found laughter to be a pain reliever. The more he laughed, the less medication he needed. Laughter, or "internal jogging" as Cousins described it, moves the focus of your attention from your pain and disability and, thus, makes room for new possibilities to emerge.

It has been said that angels fly because they take themselves lightly. Like the fabled "Hawkeye" from "M★A★S★H," we discover that laughter, a sense of humor, and hope give us a broader perspective in which the tragedies of the day may remain important, but they are no longer all-important. There is always more, for God's frontier is filled with surprises. In God's abundance, our limits give birth to new and unexpected possibilities.

Fourth, *reframe your pain and suffering.* Your pain and suffering are real, but are not the only reality. Hidden within your struggles are unexpected possibilities for growth and personal transformation. As we stated earlier, this is the wisdom of the Hebraic experience of the Passover and exodus. When there is apparently no way out, God parts the sea, helping us surmount life's obstacles and leading us to liberation. This is also the spirit of the cross of Jesus the healer. Beyond pain and agony, there is the resurrection power of new life.

In difficult times, we can choose to reframe our experience. We can focus on the deeper meaning of suffering and its role in personal growth. While illness is not God's will or the result of Divine punishment, God is still at work even in illness to inspire you to greater wisdom, integrity, and beauty. As the Jewish-Christian teacher Paul proclaims, "In all things God works for the good" (Rom. 8:28, NIV).

Rabbi Yitzak Eizak transformed his experience of pain by seeing it as a factor in his spiritual evolution. When he was asked how he could endure the debilitating pain of a lifelong illness, he responded, "You would understand readily enough if you thought of the pain as scrubbing and soaking the soul in a strong solution. Since this is so, one cannot do otherwise than accept such pain with love and not grumble. After a time, one gains the strength to endure the present pain. It is always only a question of the moment, for the pain that has past is no longer present, and who would be so foolish as to concern himself with future pain?"[4] Like Jesus, Rabbi Eizak found healing in awakening to the Eternal Now one moment at a time.

Biblical scholar Walter Brueggemann notes that one of the primary characteristics of the Hebraic prophet is his or her envisaging of an alternative reality to the current dismal and dehumanizing state of affairs. When illness strikes, we are challenged to become the prophets of our own experience— to imagine ourselves as agents in our own recovery, to see our immune system flushing out cancerous cells, and to claim our own power amid the pain and suffering. Presented with an apparently insurmountable object, we can reframe the situation and our own personal gifts in order to become creative agents rather than passive victims. Like the "Little Engine That Could," we can climb the steepest hill, affirming over and over, "I think I can, I think I can, I think I can."

Such reframing takes all the imagination we can muster when we are facing the ravages of physical pain. Above all, we initially need appropriate pain relief, but we also need to transform the pain into a blessing and see the suffering as an invitation to grow spiritually. Believe it or not, there are times when pain can be a friend. Pain tells us something is wrong and may protect us from greater harm. Without the warning signal of angina, for example, we might neglect going to the emergency room or making an appointment with our doctor. Pain may be a warning light, urging us to seek help in bringing our mind, body, and spirit back to a healthy state.

From a spiritual standpoint, the reality of pain reminds us that we cannot make it on our own and that the most joyful life involves creative interdependence and mutuality with God, other persons, and the nonhuman world. In connectedness to the Divine and others, we can always experience wholeness regardless of our physical condition.

When he was diagnosed with AIDS, David discovered, for the first time, the true meaning of love. He also experienced the joy that had eluded him most of his life. God's love was embodied in the meals brought by members of his church, friends' companionship during hospital stays, and the loving acceptance of his parents. David confesses, "When I discovered I was gay, I emotionally turned away from my parents and my friends from the church. I shut them out of my life, thinking they would never accept me for who I was. But, I was wrong. I shut them out, but they didn't shut me out. Now, I know how much they loved me all along. They loved me even when I didn't love them. It took an illness for me to see their love and accept their support." David was astounded when Paula, one of his friends from church, told him that he really mattered to the church. "We need you more than you need us. We need to give you our love just as much as you need to accept our care. We're all in this together. When you're sick, we're sick, too." David discovered that even when we shut God out, God does not shut us out. God provides persons and insights that help us experience a larger vision of reality in which our pain finds healing and comfort. David's illness inspired his congregation to begin an AIDS ministry and declare itself a congregation that would be "open and affirming" to persons of all sexual orientations.

This spirit of interdependence is found in Rabbi Nachman of Breslov's tale of "The Seven Beggars."[5] In terms of society's superficial standards, each of the beggars is terribly disfigured—one is blind, another hearing-impaired, a third unable to speak, one has a crooked neck, another a spinal deformity, one has no hands, and the last has no legs. Yet each one turns her or his disability into an advantage. As beggars and persons with disabilities, they know their vulnerability and interdependence. They find true happiness and prosperity in depending on God and their relationships with one another for everything important in life. They choose to be generous and expansive, despite their apparent "handicaps," by saving two orphans and supporting their marriage years later. They become persons of stature and wholeness, who experience God even in the most challenging situations. This is no denial of tragedy and disability, but an affirmation that we need to ask God to show us the blessing and advantage present even in the most difficult situations.

In times of prayerfulness, we may hear God's "still, small voice" giving us directions to life beyond the pain and suffering. In such moments, we discover that our limits are the source of possibility. What others see as disability may be the matrix from which a unique gift to the world emerges.

The experience of a life-threatening illness was the open door to new life for poet and environmental activist Gail Warner. At thirty, she went into the hospital for the investigation of a light but persistent cold. Much to her dismay, a chest Xray revealed a mass in her lung the size of an avocado. A biopsy the next day confirmed the diagnosis: an aggressive form of non-Hodgkins lymphoma. Warner recorded her experiences in a personal journal until her death nearly thirteen months after the initial diagnosis. In her posthumous memoir, *Dancing at the Edge of Life,* Warner records her determination to carve out meaning from her interrupted life. As her disease progressed, Warner writes, "I tell my friends that the first six months of cancer was my master's degree in love and life. Now I'm in the doctoral program." Even on her worst nights, as Warner faced her despair and fear of failure, she continued to seek out lessons from her suffering. Her life was a laboratory for spiritual emergence. As her pain grew worse, she notes that "this is another teaching." News of a relapse inspired her to greater dedication to living with meaning as she danced with vitality at the jagged edges of life.[6]

Gail Warner's experience reminds us that we are never alone in our suffering. The healing spirit of God moves through our emotions and thoughts even as it moves through the cells of our bodies. Regardless of our health condition, we can still say yes to life. As the popular foreign film *Life is Beautiful* proclaims, persons can live with dignity, grace, and love in the most difficult conditions. Our quest for spiritual growth and relationship with God may not achieve a physical cure—we may face death or live for years with a chronic ailment—but we may also experience a spiritual healing by embracing the wellsprings of hope and claiming our power simply to find beauty and wonder in the smallest of things.

Fifth, ***participate in social support networks.*** In describing the solitary state of the primordial Adam, Genesis affirms our need for companionship. The Jewish-Christian teacher Paul affirms that we are all part of the body of Christ, and that we are shaped by the joys and sorrows of one another (1 Cor. 12). The significance of relationships has been documented by medical research and personal experience. Mortality rates rise significantly, especially among men, after the death of a spouse. Broken hearts and loneliness may be factors in heart disease.[7] The competitiveness and mistrust of those identified with Type A behavior may be a significant risk factor in heart disease.

Medical studies show that healthy social contact improves quality of life and may increase a person's lifespan. Researchers found that women with advanced breast cancer who participated in a support group lived an average of eighteen months longer than those who did not belong to a support group. As partners in pain and transformation, participants in support groups for breast cancer shared how they coped with the disease and expressed their feelings about the impact of cancer on their personal, family, and professional lives. Their honest communication enhanced their ability to reveal their feelings to family members and health care professionals. Other medical studies have found that persons who are active in religious communities also live longer and healthier lives and respond more creatively to serious illness.

The significance of healthy social structures for disease prevention and well-being was demonstrated in what has been described as the "Roseto effect." During the 1950s and 60s, Roseto was a primarily Italian-American community in Pennsylvania, which became well known because the men of Roseto had lower rates of death from coronary heart disease than the average American male. The relationship between social cohesion and heart disease was studied at Roseto over a thirty-year period. The investigators noted that "what has been learned seems to confirm the old but often forgotten conception that mutual respect and cooperation contribute to the health and welfare of a community and its inhabitants, and that self-indulgence and lack of concern for others exhibit the opposite influences."[8] According to these researchers, social stability and connectedness may serve as a counterforce to the negative impact of other lifestyle behaviors such as diet and smoking. Conversely, studies indicate that the highest death rate from coronary disease is found in Reno, Nevada, where there is a higher percentage of outsiders and men who are divorced, single, or widowed.[9]

Religious rituals that recognize the passages of life—birth, adolescence and young adulthood, marriage, and death—provide comfort, guidance, and companionship in times of radical change. Strong and healthy family ties give us confidence that we can face life's crises, assured of our own personal competence and the support of indestructible ties that bind. Some studies also indicate that religion-based family life and dietary practices also promote better overall health than the fast-food diets and fragmented lifestyles of many American families.

In sharing with one another, we discover that we are not alone. We are not the first or only persons to deal with the physical, relational, and spiritual crises brought on by serious illness. In hearing others' stories, we see our lives from a new perspective. We may even discover resources for coping and transformation that we had not previously imagined. These support groups embody the spirit of Shalom, the healing web of life that unites body, mind, spirit, and relationships. Healthy support groups embody God's real presence in concrete realities of tears, touch, and listening.

In the mid-1980s, the Lombardi Cancer Center at Georgetown University Medical Center initiated the OPAS (Oncology Patients and Siblings) program, which matched college students with cancer-afflicted children and their siblings. With the companionship of their big brothers or big sisters, these children experience a lively world beyond hospital visits and tests. The smiles on their faces reflect a deeper healing that may surface in better health outcomes. When we connect with the essential relatedness of the universe, the energy of love that flows through our lives brings wholeness even when a cure may not be found. In the companionship of loving communities and a loving God, we take our first breaths, embraced by circles of love, and take our final breaths surrounded by those same, undying, and infinitely supportive circles of care.

Holiness and Wholeness

Judaism and Christianity proclaim the holiness of everyday life. Each word and act can transform the universe. Still, certain commitments awaken our experience of the Holy One in crises as well as in ordinary moments. The practices that promote well-being also prevent illness and provide healing energy when we are suffering from chronic or life-threatening illness. These spiritual practices, described in chapter 2 in terms of their medical impact, awaken us to the energy of love and healing that can transform any situation. Traditionally, spiritual leaders have stressed the importance of prayer, meditation, scripture, healing imagery, and affirmative faith in the transformation of our lives and the world. While these practices are as ancient as biblical spirituality, their wisdom is timeless, especially when we freely transform them to respond to the needs of people in the twenty-first century.

Yearning for God: The Path of Prayer. We are created for communion with the Divine. A Holy voice constantly echoes in our lives in sighs too deep for words. Aligned with God's presence, we experience joy and fulfillment. Apart from the Divine, our lives wither and contract. Although God is ever-present, God is also hidden. A parable from Rabbi Dov Baer expresses God's desire to be found in every situation:

> Once Rabbi Dov Baer was walking in the street accompanied by his disciples and saw a little girl hiding in an alcove weeping. "Why are you crying, little girl?" asked the rabbi. "I was playing hide and seek with my friends," replied the girl, "but they didn't come looking for me!" Rabbi Dov Baer sighed and said to his students, "In the answer and the tears of that little girl I heard the weeping of the *Shekinah*, 'and I will surely hide my face' (Deuteronomy 31:18). I, God, have hidden myself, as it were, but no one comes to look for me!"[10]

Judaism and Christianity believe that the search for God and our deepest self are identical. In finding God, we find our true peace and happiness.

The poetic words of Psalm 42 capture the essence of the prayerful search for God in the midst of crisis:

> As a deer longs for flowing streams,
>   so my soul longs for you, O God.
> My soul thirsts for God,
>   for the living God.
> When shall I come and behold
>   the face of God?
> My tears have been my food

> day and night,
> while people say to me continually,
>   "Where is your God?"
> These things I remember,
>   as I pour out my soul:
> how I went with the throng,
>   and led them in procession to the house of God,
> with glad shouts and songs of thanksgiving,
>   a multitude keeping festival.
> Why are you cast down, O my soul,
>   and why are you disquieted within me?
> Hope in God; for I shall again praise him,
>   my help and my God.
>
>   (Ps. 42:1–5)

Identified as one of the healing Psalms by Rabbi Nachman of Breslov, Psalm 42 reveals the heart of the spiritual journey— the faithful quest for God that unites hope and pain, abundance and scarcity, joy and sorrow.

Prayer is the yearning for God with our whole being. Fully open to God, we become open to ourselves and discover our pain as well as the Divine touch that will make us whole again. In prayer, we place ourselves in God's presence and open our hearts to Divine transformation. As the psalmist tells us:

> O LORD, you have searched me and known me.
> You know when I sit down and when I rise up;
>   you discern my thoughts from far away.
> You search out my path and my lying down,
>   and are acquainted with all my ways.
> Even before a word is on my tongue,
>   O LORD, you know it completely...
> Search me, O God, and know my heart;
>   test me and know my thoughts.
> See if there is any wicked way in me,
>   and lead me in the way everlasting.
>
>   (Ps. 139:1–4, 23–24)

Jesus of Nazareth invited his followers to pray boldly in recognition of the goodness of God:

> "Ask, and it will be given you; search, and you will find; knock, and the door will be opened for you. For everyone who asks receives, and everyone who searches finds, and for everyone who knocks, the door will be opened." (Mt. 7:7–8)

Our prayerful boldness is motivated by our willingness to let God lead the way in our lives. We can be bold in our prayerful affirmations because God is on our side. God not only wants the best for us, but God is providing the insight we need to discern what is for ourselves as well. Only God knows how to weave our prayers with the prayers of others to bring about a world of beauty and justice. As the Lord's Prayer proclaims, "Your kingdom come. /Your will be done, /on earth as it is in heaven" (Mt. 6:10).

Prayer is communal as well as individual. When we pray for others, we commit ourselves to their well-being and ask that God bring them the fullness of life. Our authentic prayers inspire us to actions that heal others and the world—a kind word, a hospital visit, a protest against injustice, an act of hospitality to social outcasts. With Martin Luther King Jr., we affirm that we are joined together in a "garment of destiny" in which our well-being is united with the well-being of creation.

The spirit of Jewish and Christian healing is found in the *Mi-Shebeirakh*, a traditional Jewish prayer for wholistic healing of body, mind, and spirit. On behalf of a distant person, one prays, "May God who blessed our ancestors, bless and heal _____, a sick person." The prayer continues:

> May the One Who blessed our ancestors Abraham, Isaac, Jacob, Sarah, Rebecca, Rachel, and Leah, bless and heal _____, who is ill. May the Holy One of Blessing shower abundant miracles on him/her, fulfilling his/her dreams, strengthening him/her with the power of life.

Merciful One;
restore him/her,
heal him/her,
strengthen him/her,
enliven him/her.

Send him/her a complete healing from the heavenly realms, a healing of body, and a healing of soul, together with all who are ill, soon, speedily, and without delay; and let us say, Amen!

While we believe that prayer creates a field of healing energy around ourselves and those for whom we pray, prayer is not magic or a quest for control. In prayer, we seek a wider perspective on life and our life situation. When we pray, synchronicities and surprises happen. As Divine energy pours into our lives, bodies and minds may be transformed and healed. But, even when prayer is not "successful" and when we must face continued illness or the prospect of death, we yearn simply for the guidance and presence of the Divine Companion.

The early Christian leader Paul of Tarsus prayed with all his heart for the cure of a chronic illness that had plagued him for years. But although he was able to cure others of their ailments and experience the mystical presence of God, this long-term ailment remained. In the midst of his anguish, he found a healing of the spirit that comes from companionship with God. In Paul's own words:

Three times I appealed to [God] about this, that it would leave me, but [God] said to me, "My grace is sufficient for you, for power is made perfect in weakness." So, I will boast all the more gladly of my weaknesses, so that the power of Christ may dwell in me. Therefore I am content with weaknesses, insults, hardships, persecutions, and calamities for the sake of Christ; for whenever I am weak, then I am strong. (2 Cor. 12:8–10)

Nearly two thousand years later, Rabbi Lev Yitzhak proclaimed the same trust, which comes from prayerful companionship with God.

> I do not beg you to reveal to me the secret of your ways—I could not bear it! But show me one thing; show it to me more clearly and more deeply, show me what this, which is happening at this very moment, demands of me, what you, O Lord of the world, are telling by way of it. Ah, it is not why I suffer, that I want to know, but whether I suffer for your sake.[11]

Whether we are healthy or ill, prosperous or unsuccessful, we find our true Shalom—our own enduring inner peace—when we see God in all things and all things in God. A life committed to prayer enables us to be worthy of our sufferings as well as generous and loving in our good fortune. Prayer connects us with God and our fellow creatures and invites us to seek their well-being even as we seek our own wholeness and prosperity.

The Healing Center. We are made for silence as well as action. In the midst of political and personal turmoil, Psalm 46:10 counsels us to "be still, and know that I am God." Jesus of Nazareth often went to lonely places to pray amid the challenges of his ministry of teaching and healing. Wholeness arises from a creative blend of action and receptivity, speech and silence.

Medical research has identified the impact of meditation on health and well-being. The "relaxation response," described by physician Herbert Benson, is an antidote to the wear and tear of ordinary life. Regular meditation, practiced fifteen to twenty minutes twice a day, reduces blood pressure and improves immune functioning. Meditation not only prevents illness and enhances overall well-being, but also reduces chronic pain. While once considered esoteric and irrelevant to the practice of medicine, meditation is now offered in hospital settings for stress reduction and palliation of long-term and life-threatening illnesses. For a number of years, Bruce has taught courses in meditation for stress reduction and spiritual growth for physicians and nurses at hospitals in Washington D.C., Maryland, and Pennsylvania.

Long before Benson's relaxation response, persons of all religious traditions practiced contemplative prayer, meditation, and centering prayer. Spiritual centering provides a healing center amid the storms of stress, illness, and bereavement. The simplest form of spiritual centering involves the following:

1. A comfortable position
2. Sitting quietly with your eyes closed
3. Prayerful openness to God's graceful presence and work in your life, and trust in God's care for all things
4. Focusing on a word or image that is meaningful to you
5. Returning gently to the point of focus, when distractions occur
6. Gently concluding the session

Traditional centering prayer involves focusing on a meaningful word such as "peace," "love," "Shalom," "light," "love," "Shekinah," or "Jesus." Others forms of centering involve focusing on the breath, gently observing inhaling and exhaling, experiencing the sheer silence, or imaging a particular healing color (golden light or purple) or symbol (such as the star of David or the cross).

Many persons judge their meditative practices deficient when they encounter distractions and wandering thoughts. But, any time spent in meditation deepens our spiritual lives and replenishes body and soul. As Rabbi Nachman of Breslov noted, "the person who says 'Amen' sincerely is counted as if the entire prayer has been said."[12]

Meditation is a response to God's unconditional love. God loves us and is working in our lives, even when we forget the Divine Presence. Meditation awakens us to what is always present and already at work in our lives—the infinite and loving creativity of God, intimately luring us toward wholeness and holiness.

The Living Word. Divine energy flows through all creatures, giving them light and vitality. The world in all its fullness reveals God's presence. Still, certain times and places are unique vehicles of revelation. Jewish and Christian mysticism affirm that scripture is a living word, and that the relative and finite words of scripture are undergirded by a holy vibration, echoing in all things. Liberated from the chains of stifling literalism, scripture is a lively and creative word bringing healing and wholeness to body, mind, and spirit. In awakening to the living words of scripture, we experience the Divine aim at healing that is present in all things.

Rabbi Nachman of Breslov identified ten psalms as the *Tikkun HaKalali*, the "Complete Remedy" for ills of body, mind, and spirit.[13] According to Rabbi Nachman, "if you believe you can do damage, then believe that you can also repair." The ten psalms, corresponding to the ten *Sefirot*—the ten attributes of God identified by Jewish mysticism, sometimes seen as the ten energies through which God created the universe—promote *tikkun*, or the mending of the world and the facilitation of the wholeness of individuals.

According to Rabbi Nachman, the first stage of the remedy is the *mikvah*, or ritual bath, which cleanses our imperfections and nurtures the new life within us. If a ritual bath is neither appropriate nor possible, simply pour water over your hands while invoking the words of Psalm 26:6–7:

> I wash my hands in innocence,
>   and go around your altar, O LORD,
> singing aloud a song of thanksgiving,
>   and telling all your wondrous deeds.

As you meditate on the ten psalms designated by Rabbi Nachman, open to the interplay of pain and hope in the psalms, experience the tension of human despair and Divine faithfulness. Explore what each psalm means in your life today. What insights and guidance do you find in the psalm? Let the healing presence of God permeate your being, giving you energy and hope.

While God speaks uniquely and intimately to each person, these ten healing psalms express the following insights:

Psalm 16—God guides and protects us even in times of sickness and struggle. Nothing can separate us from God's love.

Psalm 32—A life alienated from God leads to disharmony of body, mind, and spirit. Confession and self-awareness restore us to harmony, balance, and joyful companionship with God. In confession, we discover who we truly are and awaken to God's plan for our lives.

Psalm 41—We can praise God even in distress because God is faithful and will provide comfort for those who suffer. God is not distant and far off, but as near to us as our next breath. Divine intimacy mirrors Divine infinity.

Psalm 42—Although distressed and depressed, we can still seek after God, who aims for wholeness in our lives. In the depth of despair, we live in hope that the depression will lift and that once again we will be able to praise God. God's light shines in the darkness, and helps us find our way.

Psalm 59—God will deliver us from the forces that oppress and burden us. In companionship with God, we find authentic freedom.

Psalm 77—When God seems absent, we find strength through recalling the "God moments" of our lives. The Holy One who supported us in the past will support us in the future, despite present appearances.

Psalm 90—The brevity of life calls us to remember God's everlasting fidelity. In our finitude, we treasure and make holy each day. As mortal companions of a faithful God, our lives are meant to be adventures in love and spiritual growth.

Psalm 105—In giving thanks for God's faithfulness, we are delivered from being victims and passive spectators of our illnesses or the tragedies of life. Confident in God, we can act rather than simply react. We can take chances and do great things. Illness cannot defeat God's ultimate goal for your life.

Psalm 137—Singing our grief gives us hope. The thought of Jerusalem, the metaphor for the Divine fulfillment of all things, brings the promise of hope and spiritual healing. When we discover that the future is in God's hands, how can we keep from singing?

Psalm 150—All things praise God. The universe is a cathedral of beauty and praise. With every breath, let us praise God from whom all blessings flow.

Many centuries before Rabbi Nachman originated his healing approach to scripture, Benedict of Narsia formulated the practice of *lectio divina*, or holy reading, within the Christian monastic tradition. In the process of holy reading, the words of scripture become a lively and dynamic word, addressed personally to us and leading us toward wholeness and fulfillment. Holy reading invites us to read scripture in the following manner:

1. Read the scriptural verse or passage over a few times, letting it soak in.
2. Be still, simply listening to the interplay of speech and silence.
3. Identify a particular word or phrase in the scripture that speaks to your life.
4. Prayerfully repeat the phrase for several minutes. In the spirit of the Benedictine tradition, you may choose to walk as you meditatively reflect on the phrase. Gentle walking opens us to greater physical wholeness and promotes innovative understandings of ourselves and scripture.

5. Prayerfully ask what the unique meaning of this passage is for your life.
6. Ask for God's guidance in applying the scripture to your present circumstances. Does the scripture guide you to a particular action or change in your life?

For example, Tom, who was cited in chapter 2, found new direction in his life when he truly heard the words of John 5:1–9. The phrase that spoke to him was "Do you want to be made well?" In that moment, he experienced both his unique physical challenge and the more difficult question, "What are you going to do about it?" Another reader of John 5:1–9 might be challenged to transform her life by the words, "Stand up, take up your mat and walk." Still another reader might be struck by the excuses that the man made in response to Jesus' initial question and ask: "Am I also hiding from healing through my holding on to excuses and previous failures?" The healing word is always addressed to us personally, and our response to this lively word reveals our glorious creativity and uniqueness as God's beloved daughters and sons.

In following Benedict and Rabbi Nachman, we are freed from the unnecessary battles between faith and science. These battles, fought at the level of literal interpretations of scripture and science, hide the deeper message of scripture that awakens us to our own lives as children of God.

Healing Imagery. Scripture awakens our imagination and invites us to become part of the divine story. Meditative reading of Jesus' parables and Hasidic tales reminds us that each of us is a partner in the holy adventure. One life can change the world. One act can transform a person's life. Imagery opens the door to deeper dimensions of experience than everyday life. In the intersection of God's holy adventure and our lives, we discover treasures that we had not previously considered. Healing imagery can promote wellness as well as energize the movement toward healing—a wholeness of mind, body, and spirit—in times of sickness.

The following healing imagery may be used in every health condition. Many persons have found this imaginative prayer a helpful companion to their radiation or chemotherapy treatments. We suggest focusing on the healing light in part because light plays an essential role in Jewish and Christian spiritual imagery of God's presence in the world. The creation of the universe, described in Genesis, begins with God's declaration, "Let there be light" (Gen. 1:3). Jesus of Nazareth is called the light that overcomes the darkness of the world (Jn. 1:1–5). For Christians, God's true light, embodied in the Divine Word, or Christ, enlightens all persons. Jesus called his followers, then and now, "the light of the world" (Mt. 5:14–16). In Kabbalistic metaphysics, Divine light resides in all things. Our task as partners in healing the world is bringing forth the often hidden light for the well-being of ourselves and others.

In this spiritual exercise, we invite you simply to rest in God's presence, whether you are lying in bed, sitting in an easy chair or in a lotus position, or receiving a chemotherapy or radiation treatment, or about to undergo surgery. Take time to release any stress as you inhale and exhale deeply. As you observe the flow of your breath, begin to image a healing light entering your being. Experience this light filling your heart, bringing you joy and courage, and circulating through your body bringing health and wholeness. Experience the light circulating to your head—permeating your thoughts, feelings, memories, even as it relaxes your head and neck. Experience it flooding your neck and immune system, empowering the immune system to identify, capture, and flush out any unwanted cells or germs. Feel the light relaxing your shoulder blades and back, aligning your whole being with God's presence in the universe and yourself. Now, let the let shine in your lungs, and further downward through the digestive and reproductive systems. If you notice any places of discomfort, experience the light permeating and healing that part of the body. Feel the light going down your hips and legs until it is grounded in your feet. Experience this holy light surrounding your whole being, protecting you from all ill and giving you the energy to help others.

If you are receiving chemotherapy treatments, you may choose to envisage this light flowing through your body to bring wholeness during the course of the treatment. If you are receiving radiation, you may wish to imagine yourself bathed in Divine light. In healing imagery, we become partners in the Divine Imagination that seeks well-being for all things.

Breathing in God's light can be an important element in your daily spiritual path and a means of nurturing good health. In her quest for wholeness, Donna breathes in God's light for fifteen minutes each morning. She experiences the light of God preparing her for new insights and giving her new energy. Throughout the day, if she begins to feel anxious, unfocused, or fatigued, she breathes in the light of God, and almost immediately experiences new energy and centeredness. If she perceives herself coming down with a cold or other ailment, Donna focuses the light on her experience of discomfort and disease. She believes that in every self-limiting illness there is a "tipping point," a moment when health and illness stand in the balance. By practicing healing prayer, we tip the balance from illness toward well-being. Even when she comes down with a cold or flu, Donna still affirms that this healing prayer eases her symptoms and enables her to live more creatively with illness until she recovers. Donna sees this sense of peace as one of the greatest gifts of healing prayer, since she—by her own admission—is "an impatient person, who becomes quite angry whenever she can't move ahead with her life." She is learning that sometimes illness can provide an unintended Sabbath for reflection and taking stock of her life and behaviors.

Affirmative faith. Faith in God challenges us to embrace a healing vision of reality. The traditional confessions of faith or creeds of our religious traditions are meant to be a lens through which we interpret the world and our lives. Freed from narrow biblical literalism, one-dimensional rationalism, and lifeless orthodoxy, the words of creeds and scriptures create a vision of reality in which God is alive in the smallest cell and the most expansive galaxy. Affirmations change the way we think about ourselves and enable us to see ourselves from God's point of view, rather than our own limitations.

For many of us, the body is the source of our greatest physical and emotional discomfort. Even when we are physically well, we may see our bodies as burdens, as less attractive than other bodies, and unworthy of adequate care. Our own hatred of our bodies may even play a role in our susceptibility to illness and poor lifestyle decisions.

When we are sick, we often define ourselves as the passive victims of our disease or the health care system. Spiritual affirmations plant seeds of hope and empowerment that take root in new attitudes and behaviors.

We have found the following scripturally based affirmations helpful in promoting well-being and responding to illness:

I am created as a man in the image of God
(Gen. 1:26–27)

I am created as a woman in the image of God
(Gen. 1:26–27)

God is my creator and God created me "very good"
(Gen. 1:31)

Divine light enlightens my whole being and every cell
(Jn. 1:5)

My faith is making me whole
(Mk. 5:34)

My body is the temple of God
(1 Cor. 6:19)

I glorify God in my body
(1 Cor. 6:20)

Because God created me, my body is beautiful
(Gen. 1:26–27)

In sickness and health, God is with me
(Rom. 8:38–39)

Divine healing light flows through every cell in my body
(Jn. 1:1–5, Mt. 5:14)

At first glance, such affirmations may seem idealistic and
almost Pollyanna-like in their optimism. But, let us be clear
about two things:

1. Affirmations, and every other spiritual exercise, do not
   deny life's tragedies and our own suffering.
2. Affirmations are no substitute for appropriate medical
   care, especially if we are suffering from depression or other
   psychological distress, or chronic or potentially life-
   threatening illness. (As with all truly wholistic spiritual
   practices, we are counseled to integrate the best Western
   and complementary health practices with an ongoing
   commitment to spiritual transformation.)

Still, affirmations reveal a deeper aspect of reality than meets
the eye. In the spirit of Kabbalah and the wisdom of John's
gospel, we affirm that God's light shines in every life and brings
insight to every situation. Even if God appears hidden beneath
our physical, relational, and psychological suffering, the Divine
One is gently present bringing healing, wholeness, and
transformation. Affirmations enable us to experience the
deepest reality of ourselves and the world.

By connecting us with God's ever-present aim at healing,
an affirmative faith can move mountains and liberate the healing
light hidden by illness and debilitating physical condition. In
using these faith-based affirmations, we claim God's affirmation
of ourselves and embody God's aim at healing, regardless of
our life situation.

We are not alone in our quest for healing, nor are we
powerless when we face illness. God is with us, feeling our
pain and suffering, inspiring us to claim our creativity, and
inspiring physicians and other health care professionals to be
our healing companions. In every situation, God is giving us
spiritual tools for personal and collective healing and
transformation.

CHAPTER FOUR

From Burnout to Blessing

Cheryl was the successful pastor of a large suburban congregation. She was highly educated, energetic, and extroverted; her ministry was as multifaceted as she. In the course of a day, she was constantly on the go, flying from meeting to meeting and appointment to appointment. Cheryl didn't want to miss anyone or anything. Deep down, she also wondered if her professional staff and congregation could get along without her, or if she could get along without them! Her secretary noted, with more than a little irony, that Cheryl probably believed that even God couldn't get along without her.

Cheryl's breakneck pace and busy schedule seldom permitted her time for a coffee break or leisurely lunch. When she did eat lunch out, it was always a "working lunch" with colleagues or parishioners. Dinners at home were interrupted by the latest "crisis" at the congregation. At the end the day, Cheryl still felt there was always something more to be done. But with the new morning, she rushed off once more, coffee cup, PDA, and cell phone in hand, feeling a bit like the white rabbit from *Alice in Wonderland*, "I'm late, I'm late, for a very important date."

Everyone agreed that Cheryl was a great pastor, except her family! She seemed always to have enough time for a homeless family, anxious wife, or troubled teenager, but when it came to her own children and husband—they'd just have to wait in line until the current crisis had passed. Her husband lost track of the broken dates for dinners out, the interrupted vacations, and missed plays and soccer games. Every time the phone rang, the children rolled their eyes as their mother dashed to catch it, even though they had both "caller ID" and "voice mail." Vacations were interrupted by "emergency phone calls," e-mail correspondence, and unfinished work.

Lately, however, even Cheryl began to have second thoughts about her vocation as a religious leader. When she first entered the ministry, she adopted Mother's Teresa's phrase, "something beautiful for God," as her motto. Now, she realized that "so little time, so much to do" had become her overriding attitude toward ministry and her congregation. Dominated by the clock, Cheryl became a victim of "hurry sickness" that manifested itself in constant fatigue, anxiety, and stress-related illness. Once a gifted scholar, Cheryl had virtually no time for study and threw her sermons together in the wee hours of Saturday night. As she looked at her spiritual, relational, and physical life, she realized that she was running on empty!

Like Tom, whose life was turned upside down by the diagnosis of cancer, and Sol, who found himself overwhelmed by the demands of his rabbinical calling, Cheryl's fast-paced and frenetic world collapsed when she realized that her zest and vitality for service and ministry had disappeared. Exhausted and close to burnout, the once-energetic and enthusiastic pastor knew something had to change. She was committed to excellence in ministry, but could no longer minister as she had for so many years.

As she sat down with her husband, Paul, she realized that if she were to continue both as a person of faith and a minister, she needed a break—immediately! Fortunately, she was not the only one who had observed signs of burnout. Her leadership team also noticed that she had seemed unfocused, weary, cynical, and impatient in recent months. Usually good-natured, she had lost her temper several times in the last few months. After they arranged for her associates and an experienced retired pastor in the community to take on her responsibilities, the church board approved an immediate three-month sabbatical, in fact, the first one she had taken in her ten years as pastor. They also told her that she must change her work style when she returned to work later that fall.

The sabbatical was a spiritual challenge for Cheryl. What would she do when she had nothing to do? Who would she be without her pastoral identity? How could she say no to persons in pain? Would she have any worth if she couldn't be the "helper"?

Cheryl knew that she was meant to be a minister. Now, she would have to change her life if she were to continue in the ministry. She realized that this personal transformation would be slow and painful, but she knew it was necessary. Some of the changes were behavioral: Cheryl began to watch her diet and walk regularly. She spent more time with her kids and husband. Others were attitudinal: She had to internalize the reality that the world could get along without her, and that her value as a person was not based on how many people she helped or how good she was. "For years," Cheryl admitted, "I worried that I had never done enough to please God. I could preach about God's grace—God's unmerited and unconditional love for broken persons, but I could never accept grace. I could never fully believe that God loved me completely, regardless of who I am." Now, she realized that God loved her even when she wasn't on the job. Even if she failed, she would always be God's beloved daughter.

She joined this new theological insight with a renewed spiritual commitment and openness to the new behavior. This wouldn't be easy. But, when Cheryl looked at the quality of her marriage and family life, she realized that she wanted more than just a growing congregation. "Yes, I want to be healed, and I will do what it takes to have a new and healthy life—physically, spiritually, emotionally, and relationally—to be whole and to be fully present to myself and my family."

Now, amid the ongoing challenges of her vital parish, Cheryl has committed herself to a healthy professional life style. While she—like a physician—still must respond to unexpected emergencies, Cheryl now takes a real day off for rest and family life. She realizes that her staff can handle many of the things she had thought of as emergencies. Each day, Cheryl spends an hour in prayer, meditation, and study. Except on rare occasions, she never works more than three nights or fifty hours a week. She also chooses to spend one afternoon each week studying at the seminary library. And, most importantly, Cheryl has learned to say no to trivial projects and time-consuming chores. She has learned the meaning of William James's affirmation that the pragmatic meaning of God's existence is the ability to take "a moral holiday" from time to time, that is, to remember that the world doesn't depend on her, but is ultimately in the hands of the ever-creative and constantly nurturing God.

With a twinkle in her eye, Cheryl proclaims, "I have never been happier as a pastor. Now, I work less and get more done! I have learned to trust God and others enough to take care of tasks I can't do and problems I can't solve." Although she had once been a taskmaster for her professional staff, Cheryl's personal transformation has become contagious at her church. She reminds her staff to take days off and practices what she preaches by not interrupting them on their days off or at dinnertime. She also challenges her lay leaders to take regular "Sabbath time," even if it means saying "no" to the pastor!

On the brink of exhaustion and burnout, Cheryl chose to embrace a new life. Full of life and vocationally rejuvenated, Cheryl feels blessed each day and has become a blessing to others.

Prescriptions for Professionals

Not long ago, Bruce was shocked by the responses made by recent seminary graduates who participated in an online seminar on pastoral wholeness. Virtually all students admitted that they were not as physically healthy or spiritually sound as when they graduated from seminary. Once upon a time, they had a dream and had a call—to serve God and enable others to experience God's presence in their lives. Now, their dreams were dimming and their call was uncertain as they faced the daily demands and uncertain roles of pastoral leadership. The same could be said of today's rabbis as well. With the author of the Song of Solomon, many professionals confess, "They made me keeper of the vineyards, /but my own vineyard I have not kept!" (Song 1:6).

The traditional professions—medicine, law, and ministry—whose purpose is to nurture and restore order, balance, and health to the world, are now diseased. The evidence of professional dysfunction is everywhere—in rising burnout, stress-related illness, and addiction among professions; in lawsuits and accusations of professional misconduct; in the proliferation of minor forms of boundary violations; in divorce, family alienation, and loss of vitality and vision.

Many of those who are reading this book know precisely what we mean. Men or women, whether we are pastors or rabbis, or active in other professions, Cheryl's story is our own. Normal stress has become distress, and burnout is around the corner. Yet, there is hope for the professional—for the stressed-out minister, rabbi, physician, lawyer, and active lay leader. Just as certain habits and beliefs may lead to illness and distress, other habits and beliefs may also lead to health and wholeness.

In chapters 2 and 3, we described the interplay of spirituality and health, and suggested certain "prescriptions for wholeness." In this chapter, we focus more narrowly on ways that hard-working professionals can improve their health and prevent illness.

Our approach to professional well-being is oriented to wellness and wholeness. While we recognize the pervasive nature of stress-related illness and anxiety, which may lead, on occasion, to burnout and pathology, we also affirm the reality of a Counterforce to distress and dysfunction. We believe that life is essentially good, and that Divine goodness permeates every cell of our bodies and inspires every creative thought and compassionate emotion. In our time, our greatest professional challenge is to constantly rekindle the passion for excellence through mindful self-care and a commitment to integrity and excellence. We challenge you, as we challenge our medical, ministerial, and law students, with the questions, "Twenty years from now, will you be glad that you entered this profession? Will you wake up with zest and vitality and eagerness to begin the day? Will you still have a passion for your profession that adds to the joy of your relationships and promotes personal health? Will your family and closest friends rejoice that you have chosen your unique vocational path?"

Believe it or not, the challenge of stress and burnout is as old as the Bible. Moses, called to be God's agent in the deliverance of the oppressed Hebrews, changed his job description from political liberator and spiritual motivator to lawgiver, community administrator, and spiritual guide for an ongoing community. The tasks were overwhelming, and although Moses himself could not see it, he was near exhaustion. He was on the verge of losing both his health and his effectiveness as the people's leader. No doubt, he thought fatigue was the necessary outcome of leadership until his father-in-law, Jethro, brought his condition to his attention:

> The next day Moses sat as judge for the people, while the people stood around him from morning until evening. When Moses' father-in-law saw all that he was doing for the people, he said, "What is this that you are doing for the people? Why do you sit alone, while all the people stand around you from morning

until evening?" Moses said to his father-in-law, "Because the people come to me to inquire of God. When they have a dispute, they come to me and I decide between one person and another, and I make known to them the statutes of God." Moses' father-in-law said to him, "What you are doing is not good. You will surely wear yourself out, both you and these people with you. For the task is too heavy for you; you can't do it alone." (Ex. 18:13–18)

In essence, Jethro told Moses that he needed to ask for help. He also needed to give his inner circle a day off! In contemporary language, he needed to trust his subordinates enough to delegate. He needed to recognize his limitations and personal vulnerability, and embrace the essential relatedness of life. In affirming the connectedness of life and the God-given abilities of others, Moses would not only be more effective as a leader, he would also have the strength and focus to journey through the uncertainties of the wilderness with his people.

Centuries later, Jesus of Nazareth recognized his own need for solitude and the necessity of sharing responsibility with others. After a day filled with preaching, teaching, and healing, Jesus looked for a personal retreat for prayer and recreation:

At daybreak he departed and went into a deserted place. And the crowds were looking for him; and when they reached him, they wanted to prevent him from leaving them. But he said to them, "I must proclaim the good news of the kingdom of God to the other cities also; for I was sent for this purpose." (Lk. 4:42–43)

Every professional and community leader can identify with Jesus' attempt to find a place for rest and solitude. Often, the minute we seek "Sabbath time," the phone rings or someone knocks on the door with what seems in their eyes to be a crisis. In that moment we must decide between self-nurture and care for another. While Jesus constantly made himself available to persons in need, Jesus also had boundaries. He knew that his reply to the crowd would be met with disappointment and anger. But, perhaps, he also knew that if he decided to stay in town, his followers would never have the opportunity to become leaders themselves. His saying "no" to the crowd's request said "yes" to something just as important as responding to the crisis of the moment. He said "yes" to his own spiritual life and his ability to help others for the long haul, and he also said "yes" to his disciples' growing competence as teachers and healers. These "boundaries of the spirit" protected Jesus from the shadow side of success and modeled healthy professional behavior for his disciples as they began their own lives as teachers and healers.

Jesus and Moses both discovered the importance of limits and boundaries. They recognized, not without conflict and tension, the importance of communal support, self-care, and silence, both for their personal well-being and for their ability to help others. Today, as spiritual leaders and professionals, we need to embrace a spirituality of wholeness in our vocational lives. While there are many appropriate paths to wholeness from which to choose, depending on age, health condition, personality type, and profession, we focus in this chapter on three broad paths to professional well-being:

1. healing the mind through theological and attitudinal healing;
2. the transformation of time by reclaiming a spiritual Sabbath;
3. holy embodiment, by recognizing that physical and spiritual well-being are interconnected.

We recognize that stress is inevitable. In fact, a life without some form of stress—external demands or the internal quest for excellence—will seldom realize its true potential. However, we also realize that the occurrence of too many stressful events in a short period of time, or our own unhealthy attitudes toward stress, can undermine the well-being we seek for ourselves and others. Nevertheless, by following the prescriptions for wholeness found in this book, we can flourish despite the external and internal challenges that confront us.

Healing the Mind

We believe that the biblical tradition is ultimately about change and transformation. The God of Israel called Abraham and Sarah to become pilgrims in quest of a new land. Later, God liberated the captives in Egypt and led them on a forty-year adventure in the wilderness. Throughout the biblical tradition, God is viewed as constantly doing a new thing, challenging our complacency, and inviting us to new visions of ourselves and the world. In each moment, we are called to choose life and love. In the spirit of the prophetic tradition, Jesus the healer called his followers to imagine an alternative community and then bring it into existence. The Christian leader Paul captured the essence of our calling as followers of an adventurous God:

> Do not be conformed to this world, but be transformed by the renewing of your minds, so that you may discern what is the will of God—what is good and acceptable and perfect. (Rom. 12:2)

Today, medical scientists and spiritual leaders recognize the power of the mind to positively or negatively transform reality. Physicians and researchers invoke the importance of both the *placebo* and *nocebo* effects. On the one hand, our positive beliefs can lower our blood pressure, reduce pain, and strengthen the immune system. On the other hand, negative thinking can replicate the symptoms of a cold or flu, raise our blood pressure, and sap our physical energy. While we do not entirely create our realities by our positive or negative thoughts, it is clear, to paraphrase physician Kenneth Pelletier, that the mind can be both a healer and a slayer. Our beliefs can become biology and tip the balance between health and disease.

Spiritual wholeness depends on reclaiming what it means to be a "professional." To be a professional means to "profess" or "believe" something that shapes our character and behavior. Sadly, often our deepest beliefs are at odds with our formal confessions of faith. In fact, while many of us proclaim the existence of a benevolent and loving God, we act as if God does not truly exist when it comes to the way we live our daily lives. Or we may believe that God will punish us if we don't work hard enough or achieve perfection in our tasks. Truly our faith can cure or kill us. Just think a moment about negative beliefs that people may have about the nature of reality and their own personal existence. The stories of Cheryl and Moses suggest certain negative beliefs that may, if held over time, lead to distress and burnout:

- I am unworthy of love.
- My worth is based on my productivity.
- I must earn the love I receive from God and others.
- I am the only one who can do the job. Others are either undependable or incompetent.
- If I ask for help, people will take advantage of my weakness.
- I am alone in the world, where I cannot depend on God or others.
- I cannot afford to rest or take a holiday.
- God requires me to be constantly vigilant and active. I can never let down my guard.

Such dysfunctional views of God and ourselves share certain primary characteristics—they are highly individualistic and promote personal isolation; they deny vulnerability and interdependence; and they assert that love is conditional, that our personal worth is based on our productivity and achievement. While we have not invoked the word *sin* in this book so far, it is clear that dysfunctional understandings of reality reflect the sins of alienation—we are alone in the world and do not require others for our well being—and pride—we alone can do the job; everyone else, including God, is incompetent. Dysfunctional beliefs eventually lead to loneliness, isolation, anxiety, and distress. They are negative messages that limit our potential and depress our immune and cardiovascular systems.

In contrast, the vision of reality that we advocate in this book is grounded in a dynamic, hopeful, and open-ended relatedness, which inspires us to trust God and others to support our deepest needs. Cheryl and Moses found wholeness through "attitudinal healing"—a change of perspective on life. This change enabled them to receive as well as give, to trust God for responding to their deepest needs, to ask for other people's help, and to empower others to become leaders and professionals themselves.[1]

In a God-filled universe, we do not need to be in control of reality. While God calls us to be responsible for our actions, the Holy One also reminds us that we can safely rest in Divine Love. Faith in God challenges us to trust others to step in when we are unable to do the job by ourselves. We can rest calmly, knowing that God is constantly calling persons to be our partners in mending the world.

This dynamic and interdependent partnership is at the heart of the Hebraic image of Shalom and the Christian image of the "body of Christ." We can trust others to support us because we live in communities of giftedness and vocation.

> Indeed, the body does not consist of one member but of many. If the foot would say, "Because I am not a hand, I do not belong to the body," that would not make it any less a part of the body. And if the ear would say, "Because I am not an eye, I do not belong to the body," that would not make it any less a part of the body. If the whole body were an eye, where would the hearing be? If the whole body were hearing, where would the sense of smell be?...If all were a single member, where would the body be? As it is, there are many members, yet one body. The eye cannot say to the hand, "I have no need of you," nor again the head

to the feet, "I have no need of you."...If one member
suffers, all suffer together with it; if one member is
honored, all rejoice together with it. (1 Cor. 12:14–17,
19–21, 26)

A healthy vision of reality affirms that within the intricate
ecology of life we all need one another, and our affirmation of
interdependence reveals strength rather than weakness. Because
we are all gifted, not only can we explore our own talents, but
we can also let others grow in their personal gifts by allowing
them to share with us, and even take our place when
appropriate.

In chapter 3, we described the healing power of affirmations.
In order to heal ourselves from negative images of ourselves and
the world, we may choose to repeat the following theological
affirmations, or others that describe our spiritual journey:

God loves me unconditionally.

I see the gifts of others and help them bring them forth.

I trust God to support my efforts and send persons to be
my partners in mending the world.

I am a child of God, infinite in worth, regardless of my
physical condition or productivity.

I love myself enough to take time for self-care.

Whether I succeed or fail, I am in God's hands.

I ask for help when I need it, knowing that God will
bring the right persons into my life.

In seeing the gifts of others, I discover my own gifts.

Giving and receiving are interrelated. I am open to
receiving as well as giving.

I affirm my relatedness to all life.

Our theology, or beliefs about God and the world, can
cure or kill us! A hopeful, relational theological vision not
only opens us to God's abundant life and constant creativity,

but also awakens the wellsprings of health within our lives and inspires us to become partners with God and our creaturely companions in healing the world.

The Transformation of Time

Those of you in midlife or older may remember a segment of the Sunday evening news program *The Twentieth Century.* Toward the end of its run, the predecessor to *Sixty Minutes* began to prognosticate about what life would be like in the twenty-first century. Both authors remember one particular segment of the program in which the anchor, Walter Cronkite, mused about what persons in the twenty-first century would do with all their leisure time. He supposed that with all the labor-saving devices the twenty-first century would bring, people would have endless time for travel, recreation, and time with family.

Cronkite's dream of leisure has become a nightmare for many of us in the twenty-first century. The technology intended to simply our lives has made them more complex. What was meant to liberate us from the prison of nine-to-five jobs has trapped us in a twenty-four/seven world in which we must be in constant contact with our coworkers and clients or be left behind.

Just think of the following image of a family vacation. The family of four heads out to the beach for a two-week holiday, armed with cell phones, PDAs, beepers, and laptops. Walking on the beach, the parents simultaneously check their business messages and make essential calls to the office. Beepers hang from their bathing suits! Several times a day, they check and respond to critical e-mail messages. They may even receive several cell phone calls each day simply to keep them abreast of happenings at work. Not to be left behind, their children repeatedly answer phone messages from friends back home and relay instant e-mail messages throughout the day. You can run, but you can't hide, from the demands of the office and your own need to be connected.

The words of Psalm 46:10, "Be still, and know that I am God" and Jesus' counsel to "Come away to a deserted place all by yourselves and rest" (Mk. 6:31) seem like prescriptions for failure today! Yet, physicians remind us that our attitudes toward time can also be a matter of life and death. Just think about it: Most of our stress is time-related. Overbooked and overwhelmed by the demands of the day, many of us suffer from "time" or "hurry sickness."

The biblical tradition proclaims that the primary antidote to stress-and-hurry sickness is the Sabbath. In a world of busyness, we need to pause awhile, let go of our need to be in control and prove our personal worth by our actions, and trust God to supply our deepest needs.

> Remember the sabbath day, and keep it holy. Six days you shall labor and do all your work. But the seventh day is a sabbath to the LORD your God; you shall not do any work—you, your son or your daughter...For in six days the LORD made heaven and earth, the sea, and all that is in them, but rested the seventh day; therefore the LORD blessed the sabbath day and consecrated it. (Ex. 20:8–10a, 11)

According to biblical wisdom, even the Holy One chooses to take a sabbatical. A constantly meddling God would stifle creaturely freedom. Though God is omnipresent and omniactive, Divine Creativity is grounded in a holy absence that creates an open space for creation's children to grow and play and explore their own creative possibilities. Biblical wisdom suggests that God is not codependent, but responds in a way that honors our freedom and responsibility while challenging us to new and creative behavior.

The Sabbath proclaims that time is the moving image of eternity. Time can be our friend. The passing of time brings the gift of the seasons of life, the possibility of letting go of the past and embracing the joy of the present, and exploring the adventure of the future. Mortality itself can be gift. Despite our feelings of anxiety, the reality of death reminds us to seize each precious moment and commit ourselves to leaving something of value to the next generation. Time brings healing—of wounds, memories, grief.

The biblical tradition speaks of time in terms of *chronos* and *kairos*. Chronos is clock and calendar time. While the regular passing of time brings with it holidays, birthdays, seasons, and anniversaries, it can also trap us in deadlines and feelings of scarcity. *Kairos,* in contrast, points to abundance and scarcity, God's eternal now in which new possibilities are constantly emerging. In *kairos*, time is holy, dynamic, full, and healing. With the dawn of each day, *kairos* time inspires us to proclaim, "This is the day that [God] has made; /let us rejoice and be glad in it" (Ps. 118:24).

According to the Jewish spiritual guide Rabbi Abraham Joshua Heschel, the Sabbath is the "sanctuary of time," which enables us to experience holiness moment by moment. Each moment reflects God's inspiration and care. Each passing moment is a holy moment that can bring surprise, miracle, and transformation. Though time is "perpetually perishing," to quote the philosopher Alfred North Whitehead, the days of our lives are also treasured eternally by the One to whom all hearts are open and all desires known.

Time can renew as well as deplete. When we live by scarcity, we are overwhelmed by the stresses of the day, and we never have enough time, money, energy, or love. But, when we live by God's abundance, we always have enough to flourish in every aspect of our lives, even when external realities appear to be limited. A good night's sleep leaves us refreshed to face the challenges of a new day. Meditation for fifteen minutes renews our spirits and fills our minds with creative ideas.

Still, one of life's greatest spiritual temptations is to live by scarcity, even though God's abundance is constantly replenishing us. Only a short time after God delivered them from captivity in Egypt, the children of Israel began to doubt God's providential care. They even wanted to go back to the apparent security of servitude, if it meant square meals and a place to stay.

> The Israelites said to them, "If only we had died by the hand of the LORD in the land of Egypt, when we sat by the fleshpots and ate our fill of bread; for you have brought us out into this wilderness to kill this whole assembly with hunger." (Ex. 16:3)

Despite their faithlessness, God was committed to providing the children of Israel with bread for the journey.

> Then the LORD said to Moses, "I am going to rain bread from heaven for you, and each day the people shall go out and gather enough for that day."…In the evening quails came up and covered the camp; and in the morning there was a layer of dew around the camp. When the layer of dew lifted, there on the surface of the wilderness was a fine flaky substance, as fine as frost on the ground. (Ex. 16:4, 13–14)

As we read the story, we believe that God had already provided the quail and manna, but the people were so caught up in the spirit of scarcity that they were oblivious to God's abundant care. When we are connected to the Holy One, we have all the time and energy we need.

Whether we speak about finances or time, the stresses of life diminish when we trust God to supply our deepest needs. As Jesus proclaimed, "I came that they may have life, and have it abundantly" (Jn. 10:10). This is a metaphysical as well as personal statement of faith.

But, how do we transform time—and our lives as a whole—from scarcity to abundance, and from a series of "deadlines" to a wealth of "lifelines"? What practical measures can we take to make time a friend rather than an enemy? The primary antidote to "time sickness" involves doing what comes naturally—breathing. Breath is God's gift to humanity. In breathing on the dust of the earth, God brought forth living beings. In breathing on his disciples, Jesus gave them God's Holy Spirit. Our breathing reflects the quality of our emotional lives. Shallow, frantic breath mirrors our own personal stress and panic. In contrast, gentle, full breaths reveal a sense of calm and inner peace. Mindfulness about the breath of life brings peace of mind and spiritual centeredness.

Spiritual guide Alan Armstrong Hunter invited his students to "breathe the spirit deeply in" and exhale any anxiety or stress that they might be feeling. The practice is a simple one: Whether walking or sitting, begin simply to breathe. Feel the gentle air enter your being, bringing life and vitality. Then with each new breath, say the words:

"I breathe the Spirit deeply in."

Exhaling, simply experience yourself letting go of any stress or burden with the words,

"I blow it gently out again."

Whenever you find yourself feeling anxious, stop a moment and breathe. As you mindfully attend to your breath, you may discover that you can find peace of mind at any moment. You also may experience a spiritual fullness even on the most demanding days.

We can reverse the "fight–or–flight response" by breathing our prayers throughout the day. We may even discover that our whole lives become a prayer as we embrace the Divine Spirit with every breath. Breathing with the Spirit, each breath can be a Sabbath!

Simplicity of life is not a matter of withdrawal from life, but centeredness and renewal in the midst of life. One of the busiest persons the authors know proclaims that he really only does *one* thing amid his many tasks—serve God and support the growth of others. His approach to life incarnates the wisdom found in Stephen Covey's affirmation, "Begin with the end in mind." While multitasking is unavoidable for many of us, our commitment to prayerfulness can bring harmony, balance, and integrity to the complexities of life. Further, when we live prayerfully, we naturally begin to discern the difference between the important and the inessential. Our true priorities rise to the surface and become the center around which we plan our days.

One helpful way of prioritizing and simplifying our lives is the practice of letting interruptions call us to prayer. When the phone rings or someone knocks at the door, say a brief prayer, such as, "Let me see God in this situation," or "I will give and receive love in this situation." We can also make a commitment to pray through our calendars and schedules. Bruce looks at the day ahead and asks God to be present at each appointment. In the space between each appointment, he takes a moment to breathe deeply, take a stroll up the hall or outdoors, and pray for the next meeting, asking that he be aware of God's light in the person and situation that will confront him. If he expects the meeting to be challenging in nature, he surrounds himself in God's healing and protective light, and then surrounds each of the participants in that same Divine light.

The Wisdom tradition of scripture challenges us to "number our days." Today, this means to live in God's presence throughout the day and to see holiness and beauty in each thing. Theologian Patricia Adams Farmer challenges us to take "beauty breaks" throughout the day. Just as lovely vistas promote healing for hospitalized persons, regular beauty breaks enlarge our spirits and put the challenges of each day in perspective.[2] No doubt Jesus had this in mind when he invited his followers to bathe their spirits in "the eternal now" of Divine artistry:

> "Therefore I tell you, do not worry about your life, what you will eat or what you will drink, or about your body, what you will wear...Look at the birds of the air; they neither sow nor reap nor gather into barns,

and yet your heavenly [Parent] feeds them…Consider
the lilies of the field, how they grow; they neither toil
nor spin, yet I tell you, even Solomon in all his glory
was not clothed like one of these…But strive first for
the kingdom of God and his righteousness, and all these
things will be given to you as well." (Mt. 6:25a, 26a,
28b–29, 33)

Try the following spiritual practice some time when you
are feeling particularly harried. Leave your desk or computer
terminal and take a walk outdoors. Even in the city, you can
find something lovely to gaze upon for a few minutes. With
the Native Americans, biblical spirituality affirms, "with beauty
all around us, we walk."

Sabbath keeping is a matter of attitude and perception rather
than legalistic rules. Renewal and growth are essential to reality,
from the atomic to the interstellar. Yet, the ever-flowing,
dynamic energy of the universe can be blocked by our attitudes,
behaviors, and priorities. As Jesus noted, the Holy One's energy
flows through us like sap from the vine to its branches.
Disconnected from Divine energy, we physically wither and
spiritually die. But, connected to the vine, abiding in God's
everlasting life, we "bear much fruit" and provide sustenance
to others (Jn. 15:5).

Renewal consultants Suzanne Schmidt and Krista Kurth
remind us that "running on plenty at work" can characterize
our professional lives when we commit ourselves to personal
revitalization.[3] Holy work can be rejuvenating and inspiring
rather than fatiguing and boring. Sabbath keeping is the most
fundamental form of renewal.

Each day can become a holy day through prayerful living,
beauty breaks, mini-Sabbaths, centering and breath prayer, and
abundant living. But, we must also plan for the long haul. Life
is both a sprint and a marathon. Some days, we must rush from
one meeting to another, or fly from one task to the next, holding
our center by prayer and healing breath. We carry a cathedral

within that we can invoke at any time. But, wholeness for the journey comes when we commit ourselves to regular and extended times of rest, retreat, holiday, and prayer. We need extended times of quiet to refresh our spirits and awaken us to Divine inspiration.

We are children of eternity, connected with the birth of the universe, the formation of the planets and solar systems, and the rise of the ecosphere. In this holy moment, God's everlasting life speaks through us and leads us toward an unimagined future. We have enough time for love, rest, work, and play, because this sacred second of life springs forth from the creativity of the Living and Eternal One and returns home to the everlasting Memory of God.

Holy Embodiment

Judaism and Christianity are profoundly embodied religions. Jesus healed the sick, in part, because he knew the vital and intimate interplay between spiritual and physical well-being. Creation in all its wonder and diversity reflects Divine love and intelligence. Human life is the moment-by-moment creative synthesis of cells, organs, nerves, emotions, thoughts, dreams, and imagination, along with the inflowing of the creaturely and Divine environment. All things, body and soul, are words of God, reflections of the Divine light that shines through every cell and thought. Even the forgetfulness of the luminous sparks and creatures who turn from darkness to light, described respectively by Isaac Luria, and the author of John's gospel, cannot stifle the healing movements of omnipresent Divine Wisdom.

Eco-theologian Thomas Berry speaks of the universe as the primary revelation of God. Yet, although many of us rejoice at God's beauty in the stars above, the Rocky Mountains, and Pacific sunsets, we are often oblivious and scornful of the most intimate revelation of Divine artistry, the dynamic mind-body partnership that animates our lives. Take a look in the mirror right now; explore the intricate uniqueness of your face and observe—regardless of your age or physical condition—the wonder of your body and the various systems within it.

Christians and Jews alike affirm that spirit is embodied and the body inspired. The twin New Testament affirmations—"the Word became flesh" (Jn. 1:14) and "your body is a temple of the Holy Spirit" (1 Cor. 6:19)—reflect the deepest intuitions of both Judaism and Christianity. The apostle Paul challenges his readers to "glorify God in your body" (1 Cor. 6:20). Two thousand years later W. H. Auden felt the need to remind us to "love God in the world of the flesh." Indeed, we best love the Creator by loving the creatures: first of all, that most intimate creature, that inspired body that we call ourselves, and then the reflections of the Creative One in the world around us.

Recently, a young pastor objected to the self-care focus of Bruce's course on Wholeness in Ministry. "Isn't this too self-centered?" he complained. "Shouldn't we dedicate our lives to serving others, regardless of the cost? The interest in self-care seems like self-indulgence to me." Bruce gently responded, "Yes, we are called to serve others. But, remember what the flight attendant says, 'Put on your oxygen mask before you place one on your child's face.' If you don't take care of yourself, you eventually won't be able to care for others. Remember what Jesus said, 'Love your neighbor as yourself.'"

In the intricate ecology of life, appropriate self-care contributes to the well-being of others. When we are stressed-out and fatigued, we easily become impatient, angry, and insensitive to the needs of others. Just remember the last time you lost your temper with a coworker, loved one, or perfect stranger. No doubt at some point that day, you also lost your spiritual center. The world became a place of scarcity and fear. Alienated from the Divine love in your own life, you were unable to share your love with others. Just look at the weary and impatient father yelling at his child in the supermarket. A few moments of rest, meditation, play, or exercise beforehand, as well as a better sense of the rhythm of the child's life, are often the best antidotes to many ordinary parent-child conflicts.

When we don't take care of ourselves physically, we are unable to respond to the deepest needs of others. Studies indicate that ministers and rabbis who regularly work more than fifty hours a week have a higher incidence of physical exhaustion, relational dysfunction, and spiritual emptiness. Professional misconduct is correlated with poor self-care, which leads to boundary violations. These maladies also apply to overworked stay-at-home moms and dads and their professional spouses.

Healthy embodiment is a matter of mindfulness. In the previous chapters, we presented various prescriptions for healing and wholeness of mind, body, and spirit. These prescriptions, which apply to every profession and station in life, essentially come to spiritual awareness of our daily needs, which is reflected in healthy work, relational, and lifestyle behavior. Fundamentally, the Sabbath that renews the mind is at the heart of healthy embodiment. Well-being of body, mind, spirit, and relationships is nurtured and renewed by a life of activity and challenge that is grounded in prayer, exercise, rest, friendship, and healthy eating.

We are made for movement. Healthy embodiment involves dancing our faith with movements appropriate to our physical condition. There is no one type of exercise suitable for all persons. Indeed, the best exercise program is one that you enjoy and can easily practice in your particular living or work context—whether it is regular walking, skating, running, yoga, weight-training, or swimming. The key is to see your exercise program as a manifestation of God's presence in your life and your own self-love. In this way, exercise becomes a blessing rather than a task.

We are created to touch and be touched. Healing touch—whether Reiki touch healing, massage, laying of hands, cuddling, caressing, or making love—connects us to the universe and the infinite supply of Divine energy that constantly sustains us. We are also created for the Sabbath rest, which, in its many forms, reflects the need to balance action with silence, sleep with wakefulness, light with darkness, focus with ambience, and communion with solitude.

For us as professionals, our beliefs are embodied and, in the intricate ecology of life, our bodies also inspire us to health or illness. God's aim for us is abundance in every aspect of our lives. Although the abundant life takes many forms and may be achieved through many paths, the Holy One calls us to choose constantly on the side of life, rather than death, so that the Divine light might shine through us, leading others to the wholeness and vitality that will glorify God in their own lives.

CHAPTER FIVE

The Healing God

Author Madeleine L'Engle tells the story of a parent who tried everything to comfort her sleepless child. After nothing seemed to work, the parent invoked an abstract theological concept to calm her child, "Don't be afraid, dear, God will be with you." In response, the child replied, "I know that, Mommy, but I want somebody with skin on."

Biblical spirituality affirms the importance of embodiment. God created the physical world in all its variety, and affirmed that it was "very good." Jesus' touch mediated the Divine energy of love to sick and dying people. The prophets and Jesus proclaimed a holy materialism in which the sharing of bread transformed hearts as well as bodies. The God of Israel, of the early Christians, and of today's Jews and Christians seeks healing and wholeness not only of our spirits and emotions, but also of our bodies and relationships.

Throughout this book, we have affirmed that our beliefs can make the difference between health and sickness. What we believe about God, ourselves, and others shapes every aspect of our lives and influences our social and political behavior. Our compassionate thoughts and prayers radiate across the universe, creating a healthy field of force that may even influence the well-being of others. Although we have focused on promoting well-being and responding to illness, every page, implicitly or explicitly, has revealed our affirmation of a lively and intimate God who seeks abundant life for all creation.

Any discussion of God's nature must be grounded in the humble recognition of our intellectual and spiritual limitations. Everything we say about God contains an explicit affirmation and an implicit denial. Progressive Judaism and Christianity recognize, first, that God is revealed in all things. The heavens declare the glory of God and so do the cells of our bodies. God is found in the breaking of bread and the loving touch that transforms. Divine inspiration guides the medical researcher, the physicist, and the crossing guard. While all places and persons reveal the Holy One, certain sites and individuals may become the unique media for God's constant communication to humankind—Jerusalem, Iona, sages, prophets, wise women and men, Abraham, and Jesus of Nazareth. Despite God's universal revelation, it is equally clear that no creature can fully experience or describe the Divine. Even our deepest beliefs must come with a warning: If you think you understand it fully, it isn't God.

Progressive Christians and Jews challenge idolatry in all its forms. On the one hand, an idol is any finite creature that demands absolute obedience and claims infallibility, whether that creature is a nation, political figure, spiritual leader, or sacred book. On the other hand, any doctrine, ritual, or sect becomes an idol when it requires unconditional belief. Whatever cannot be questioned is an idol, dangerous to the health of the body as well as the mind. Progressive Jews and Christians are spiritual agnostics, who recognize that open-hearted and open-minded doubt is essential to discovering the truths that heal. With the early Christian teacher Paul, we recognize, "now we see in a mirror, dimly, but then we will see face to face. Now I know only in part; then I will know fully, even as I have been fully known" (1 Cor. 13:12).

Envisaging the Healing God

Despite the inherent limitations of all images of God, we believe that the nature of reality and the insights of the biblical tradition allow us to describe the healing God with the following affirmations. In the spirit of a Zen Buddhist saying, these affirmations point toward the Divine, but are not the Divine itself. The Holy Adventure is always lively, dynamic, and surprising. God is always more than we can imagine.

First, the healing God is defined primarily by love and compassion. The biblical tradition affirms that God's mercy and loving kindness endure forever. While certain biblical passages describe God in terms of power, justice, and vengeance, the healing God is ultimately experienced in terms of God's deliverance of the oppressed, forgiveness of the wayward, care for the vulnerable, and love for the lost. The biblical tradition can be seen as the often painful and challenging quest to discover a God whose stature and love can embrace the world in all its suffering and complexity. The one true God embraces friend and foe, healthy and sick, insider and outsider.

Inspired by the the prophet Isaiah's image of the suffering servant and the life and teachings of Jesus the healer, the early Christians proclaimed that authentic spirituality begins and ends in companionship with a loving God.

> Beloved, let us love one another, because love is from God; everyone who loves is born of God and knows God. Whoever does not love does not know God, for God is love…No one has ever seen God; if we love one another, God lives in us, and [God's] love is perfected in us. (1 Jn. 4:7–8, 12)

Everything we say about God's nature and relationship to the world finds its meaning in terms of God's love for creation. God's power is loving power; God's justice is loving justice;

God creativity is love in action. God's love, embodied in sages, saints, and healers, is the model for human love. The world in all its diversity was created by Love. The world finds its unity and healing in Love.

Whereas certain philosophers and theologians see Divine perfection in terms of Divine immutability and immunity from the world of pain and suffering, progressive Judaism and Christianity see God's perfection in terms of an intimate creative and responsive love. God is, as the Episcopalian Book of Common Prayer states, "the One to whom all hearts are open and all desires known."

God hears our prayers, feels our pain, and rejoices in our success. Our lives truly make a difference to God. God is a different God because of our prayerful acts of kindness and healing. God's experience of the world is enhanced by the creativity and love of God's creaturely children.

Rabbi Abraham Joshua Heschel describes God's relationship to the world as the Divine pathos.

> The divine pathos points to a connection between God and [humankind] – a connection which originates with God. God "looks" at the world and its events. [God] experiences and judges them; this means that [God] is concerned with [humankind] and somehow related to [God's] people. The basic feature of divine pathos is God's transcendental attention to [humans].[1]

Our lives are our gifts to God. As Jesus taught his disciples, "as you did it to one of the least of these who are members of my family, you did it to me" (Mt. 25:40).

Centuries later, Mother Teresa saw the heart of spirituality in terms of doing something beautiful for God.

Contemporary theologians describe God's love in terms of panentheism, the affirmation that all things are in God, and God is in all things. Only a panenetheistic God can love us, hear our prayers, and heal our suffering. The Divine pathos is revealed in Dietrich Bonhoeffer's affirmation that "only a suffering God can save." Despite its constant waywardness, God still loves Israel and longs for its companionship:

When Israel was a child, I loved him,
    and out of Egypt I called my son.
The more I called them,
    the more they went from me;
they kept sacrificing to the Baals,
    and offering incense to idols.

Yet it was I who taught Ephraim to walk,
    I took them up in my arms;
    but they did not know that I healed them.
I led them with cords of human kindness,
    with bands of love.
I was to them like those
    who lift infants to their cheeks.
    I bent down to them and fed them...

How can I give you up, Ephraim?
    How can I hand you over, O Israel?...
My heart recoils within me;
    my compassion grows warm and tender.
                    (Hos. 11:1–4, 8)

Like the shepherd of Jesus' parable, God searches for every lost soul until it is found and brought home to its true resting place. Human freedom is real and shapes the character of Divine activity, but God's love is infinite, unending, and adequate to every life situation. While we cannot fully imagine the nature of God's inner life, we can affirm the intimate images of Rabbi Meir:

When [a human] is sorely troubled, what says the *Shekinah?*

My head is ill at ease, my arm is ill at ease.[2]

Still, we need a God with skin on! God's love is cosmic, but it is equally intimate. When we say that God loves the world enough to suffer and rejoice in it, what we truly affirm is that "God loves me!" and, more radically, "God (also) loves my enemy!" God seeks healing and abundant life out of God's great compassion for all creation in its pain and joy.

Second, God is intimately related to all things. The meaning of Divine omnipresence is simply that God is with us. Nearer to us than ourselves, God's still small voice speaks within us in sighs too deep for words. God breathes within our every breath. From birth to death, God is our closest companion, "the Fellow Sufferer who understands."

> Where can I go from your spirit?
>   Or where can I flee from your presence?
> If I ascend to heaven, you are there;
>   if I make my bed in Sheol, you are there.
> If I take the wings of the morning
>   and settle at the farthest limits of the sea,
> even there your hand shall lead me,
>   and your right hand shall hold me fast.
> If I say, "Surely the darkness shall cover me,
>   and the light around me become night,"
> even the darkness is not dark to you;
>   the night is as bright as day,
>   for darkness is as light to you.
>   (Ps. 139:7–12)

God can respond to our deepest needs because God alone knows us as we truly are. Jesus the healer responded to each person's need intimately. He treated each one as if he or she were the *only* one, and provided a way that would lead to each one's own unique healing and transformation.

God's power is revealed in the Divine listening that empowers creation to become what it is meant to be. Yet, the Divine listening also enables God to "speak" to our personal life situation.

Divine activity and Divine receptivity are woven together in God's care for each creature. God appears to each person in terms of her or his deepest need and personal situation. Moment by moment, God gives each person and each cell a vision of what it can become in a world defined by beauty, love, and goodness. According to one Midrash, or biblical interpretation, God reveals God's self "according to the power of each individual, according to the individual power of the young, the old, and the very small ones."[3] There is no *one* spiritual experience appropriate to every person. Nor is there *one* form of healing and wholeness appropriate to every person. Our physical condition, spiritual life, environment, and community are the contexts within which God seeks what is best for us. At certain times, God's aim is for a physical healing through the interplay of prayer, touch, and medical care. At other times, God's deepest desire is a gentle death in the companionship of loved ones.

God is truly a personal companion, whose love reveals itself in what is best for us in all our uniqueness. As we ponder the interplay of cosmic adventure and personal intimacy, we are comforted by the affirmations that "God is working in my life to bring me wholeness and love" and "God is working in my spouse's (child's, partner's, enemy's) life to bring her or him wholeness and love." Within the unique context of our environment and personal history, God truly seeks the healing that is right for each one of us.

Third, God is constantly doing something new in my life and in the world. With God, there are no dead ends. God is constantly weaving together actuality and possibility, reality and imagination, to give birth to a world of love, beauty, and wholeness. When we imagine alternative possibilities to injustice, suffering, poverty, and emotional depression, God is our partner in envisaging novel futures and bringing them into existence.

Just think of the biblical vision of God's partnership with humankind. Abraham and Sarah are promised a new home and a child, even though they envisaged a childless retirement in their hometown. After leaving Egypt in fear and disgrace,

Moses is given a second chance to lead his people from slavery to freedom. Jesus welcomes outcasts, heals the sick, and brings hope to the hopeless. Jesus empowers the faltering Peter, who abandoned him when he most needed his companionship, to become a spiritual leader for the emerging church. Passover and Easter are God's revelations that nothing can defeat God's dream of healing and liberation.

God's aim in our life is "prophetic healing." God gives persons and communities the vision of Shalom that speaks to their gifts and needs and, then, provides the ongoing inspiration and support to realize the Divine dream of wholeness and peace. The Divine imagination inspires the hopeful imaging of a man diagnosed with cancer, the persistence of a woman attempting to change her lifestyle, and a community seeking a just health care system. As children of God's abundant life and unfettered imagination, each one of us can affirm that "God is presenting me—and everyone else—with new and lively possibilities for growth and transformation." God's healing imagination is at work in our lives, regardless of our current physical, emotional, or economic situation. Just as important, God's healing imagination is inspiring others to become our partners in the interplay of personal and global healing.

Fourth, the intimate and loving God unites personal and global wholeness and healing. The biblical vision of Shalom proclaims that all health is public health and all healing is global healing. Healthy self-care is not narcissistic and self-centered, but altruistic in nature. Authentic self-centeredness inspires us to seek the well-being of all creation. God wants each one of us to flourish; but God also aims at the healing of all creation. Jewish mysticism asserts that the healing of one soul brings healing to the whole universe. Authentic personal healing arises from and contributes to the healing of the environment. As we bring forth God's inner light in our lives, we enable others to discover their own inner light. You are light of the world. Let your light shine to give light to others!

While some people critique the growing interplay of spirituality and medicine as a reflection of today's individualistic and self-absorbed cultural environment, the vision of Shalom unites individual and social well being. From this perspective, healing prayer encompasses the planet as well as well the person. Our true healing must always be seen in light of the well-being of others. The apostle Paul's letter to the Romans presents a majestic vision of cosmic healing in which our cries for wholeness join the chorus of creation.

> For the creation waits with eager longing for the revealing of the children of God...We know that the whole creation has been groaning in labor pains until now; and not only the creation, but we ourselves, who have the first fruits of the Spirit, groan inwardly while we wait for adoption, the redemption of our bodies...Likewise the Spirit helps us in our weakness; for we do not know how to pray as we ought, but that very Spirit intercedes with sighs too deep for words. (Rom. 8:19, 22–23, 26)

The universe is a vast web of relationships in which the Divine Artist seeks to join the well-being of the whole with the well-being of each part. In this dynamic universe, freedom is real. Although limited by the influence of Divine Creativity and the multiple influences of the environment, our actions shape the web of relatedness for good or ill, health or disease. Our true happiness emerges when we join our deepest aspirations and hopes with the deepest aspirations and hopes of others, including generations of future humans and our nonhuman companions. The goal of healing is not just physical health, the cure of an illness, or personal prosperity, but the spiritual peace that arises from experiencing ourselves as members of God's holy adventure, joined with every other member of this vast, rising and perishing, reflection of Divine Creativity.

Our greatest joy arises when we experience God in all things and all things in God. As our spirits grow in stature, we can make sacrifices for the well-being of the whole and face our own mortality, knowing that we are part of an infinite holy adventure, and affirming, "Divine Love unites my life with every other life."

Fifth, God and the world exist in a dynamic partnership in which the Infinite One relies upon our loving actions to heal the world. Progressive Judaism and Christianity see our personal, planetary, and cosmic histories as dynamic and open-ended. While some Christians and Jews assert the doctrine Divine omnipotence, the belief that God is the all-powerful ruler and determiner of history, we maintain that authentic biblical spirituality reflects an ongoing partnership between God and humankind, in which finite humans shape, to some extent, not only the Divine experience but also the character of Divine activity in the world.

Divine and human love, at their best, maximize freedom and creativity in the lives of those who are loved. Further, healthy love involves the willingness to listen as well as to speak. The freedom and creativity that love affirms involves risk-taking. The future in its details is unfinished and uncertain. Although God's love guides all things toward healing, we do not expect a dramatic and unilateral second coming nor do we expect God to save us by a supernatural act from destroying our planet through global warming, greed, or biological or nuclear warfare. But what we can count on is the Divine faithfulness that will guide and support us in even the most difficult personal and planetary situations. God works within the challenges of life and the divinely influenced laws of nature to bring about the greatest beauty, love, and healing in every situation and in the planet as a whole.

Progressive Christianity and Judaism affirm that there is a gentle force working within our lives and the lives of communities and nations to promote wholeness and justice.

We also believe that we are called to be partners with this Healing Presence in mending the world.

While we must not overemphasize the significance of our actions on the cosmic plane, we are called to be God's stewards and cocreators on the earthy plane of personal health, relationships, and communities. As radical as it may seem, God needs us to be the divine partners in bringing wholeness to our world. This partnership is the source of life's adventure in all its beauty and tragedy. As Abraham Joshua Heschel asserts, "Not only is God necessary to [humanity] but that [humanity] is necessary to God, to the unfolding of God's plans in the world."[4] The *Genesis Rabbah* affirms that God envisaged a world of companionship and creativity.

> From the first day of creation, the Holy One, blessed be [God], longed to enter into partnership with the terrestrial world, to dwell with [God's] creatures within the terrestrial world.[5]

Ironically, the imperfection of our world—the pervasive injustice, suffering, and death—makes our role in healing the world more significant. Divine Creativity is hospitable by nature. God's love makes room for creaturely freedom. Although God is the most intimate influence in each moment's experience and in the cosmic adventure, each creature freely chooses, within the limitations of its past actions and current environment, whether or not it will embody God's dream for it. Cancer, AIDS, or terrorism arise from the multifaceted nature of reality and human decision-making. God is not the source of suffering and pain. Rather, God seeks our companionship in preventing suffering and disease, and responding to the injustice and pain of the world.

We are God's partners in bringing about God's will "on earth as it is in heaven." Like the flapping wings of the butterfly, our prayers radiate across the universe, creating a "healing field" that opens new possibilities for Divine and human transformation. Inspired by the Divine Companion, our actions may be the tipping point between life and death for ourselves, others, and the planet. Our actions enable God to be effective in empowering us to achieve our highest ideals. As philosopher Alfred North Whitehead asserts, "Every act leaves the world with a deeper or fainter impress of God. [God] then passes into his next relation to the world with enlarged, or diminished, presentation of ideal values."[6] Whitehead's words echo the *Pesikta*'s understanding of humankind's surprising role in God's evolving presence in the world:

> When Israel performs the will of the Omnipresent, they add to the strength of the divine power. When, however, Israel does not perform the will of the Omnipresent, they weaken, if it is possible to say, the great power of the One who is above.[7]

The healing stories of the New Testament proclaim this same partnership. Where there is faith, new possibilities emerge that can transform bodies as well as spirits. Yet, where there is no faith, the healing connection is broken, and Jesus cannot fully share God's abundance with humankind.

Our calling is to be God's joyful healers and messengers in the world today. Psalm 8 proclaims our role as shepherds and stewards of creation. "You have made [us] a little lower than God, /and crowned [us] with glory and honor" (Ps. 8:5). Hebrew Bible scholar Denise Dombkowski Hopkins notes the importance of thanksgiving and praise in transforming the world and God's own experience:

> When God is praised, and praised properly, God is the better for it. God's power becomes more focused; God's power is magnified because God allows and equips the entire universe to sing the divine praise. We praise, not just for the sake of spreading God's name among the world and among ourselves, but for God's sake as well. If our praise makes a difference for the world, then it

also makes a difference for God. Those related in worship—God, human beings, and the rest of creation—are now different from what they were before this worship of praise.[8]

Praise awakens the power of affirmative faith. In the synergy of divine and creaturely inspiration, the Psalms conclude with the affirmation of all creation, "Let everything that breathes praise [God]! /Praise [God]!" (Ps. 150:6).

In each moment, God calls us to a healing partnership. God invites us to bring light to our world by committing ourselves to self-healing and healing of the planet. God calls us to be prophetic healers, who imagine creative and novel possibilities for ourselves and for the world, and then embody these practices in our individual and community lives. As God's beloved sons and daughters, we have the power of *tikkun*, the choice to restore the original wholeness of the world in terms of our time and place—to embody God's dream for healing in our time.

CHAPTER SIX

Walking in the Light of God

During the time of the worst oppression in South Africa, churches were often suspected of treason against the Afrikaner government. Pastors were especially at risk because they proclaimed that all persons, even oppressed Africans, were holy children of God, created in the Divine image and called to full partnership with God and humankind. Many religious leaders were arrested and tortured by the South African police force. Knowing the risk of taking a stand against injustice, on many Sunday mornings, the congregation would gather outside the pastor's home and accompany the pastor to church, joyfully singing over and over the words:

> We are walking in the light of God!
> We are walking in the light of God!
> We are walking in the light of God!

In the darkness of apartheid, they proclaimed that hatred and oppression could never quench the light of God. They knew that as long as they sang and prayed together, they would be safe from harm. God's protective and healing light would outlast any force that might threaten them. And it did![1]

In the worst of evils, the most severe suffering and pain, we can walk in the light of God. The healing light that promotes well-being also gives hope and comfort to persons in pain. This affirmation has been our message throughout this book. Although darkness may hide the husks, the unquenchable light of God shines forth from within each creature. This omnipresent and transforming light brings healing to the sick and comfort to the dying. It inspires our commitment to join individual and communal well-being in our quest to bring wholeness and healing to our world.

Progressive Judaism and Christianity affirm that the light of God is the deepest reality of all things. With the healer Jesus, we proclaim that each person is an expression of the Divine Light, a manifestation of the creative and life-transforming energy of love. Nothing can hide that light once it has been discovered! It shines on a hilltop guiding the path of every passerby.

In the spirit of the teachings of Jesus and the metaphysics of the Kabbalah, our task is to raise the light—to redeem the world by bringing forth the light in others and awakening to our own inner light. When Bruce was a child, growing up in the Baptist church, his Sunday school class often sang, "This Little Light of Mine," including the verse, "Everywhere I go, I'm gonna let it shine." That is our task today: to let our light shine to give light to a world often locked in the darkness that is physical, emotional, spiritual, and relational. As progressive Christians and Jews, we know that we need one another in order to fully actualize the healing possibilities that lure us forward. Together we can see the light and bring forth the unexpected possibilities hidden in every crisis. Much to our surprise, we are discovering that God needs us to be partners in healing the earth. We are God's light bearers and health givers.

The "husks" of life can easily hide the beauty and wonder of our world. Sickness, pain, and suffering can dim the light of God and dominate our experience of reality. Unhealthy habits can imprison us and dominate our lives. The world can shrink to the size of the hospital room. The prospect of our own death or the death of a loved one can paralyze us and deaden our spirits.

The recognition of the reality of pain and suffering is at the heart of both Christianity and Judaism. But, progressive Judaism and Christianity proclaim a deeper vision of reality, the reality that God's original and indestructible wholeness embraces and transforms the darkness of life in all its forms. Life involves risk, for God and for ourselves, but within life's evolving adventure, the Holy One provides novel images of healing and transformation and the energy to embody them in our lives and communities. In the shining light of God, the sick are healed and find peace and comfort.

Condemned to servitude under the Egyptian yoke, the Hebrew slaves saw nothing but entrapment as they peered into the future. But in their anguish, they discovered that God is faithful. God heard their prayers and made a way to freedom where the path once was blocked. Abraham and Sarah feared they would die childless until God heard their prayers and gave them a child and a new land. The sick and forgotten saw no hope for themselves until they saw themselves through the eyes of the healer Jesus and claimed the healing of mind, body, spirit, and relationships that was God's dream for their lives. The rock that sealed the tomb of Jesus imprisoned the spirits of Jesus' followers until the glorious day of resurrection.

Progressive Christianity and Judaism affirm that a force of healing and wholeness moves through all things. We see traces of its power in the healing of the wounds of body, mind, and spirit, and the reconciliation of those who have been estranged. We experience it in the unfettered imagination that lures us to new adventures. That gentle force calls us to be its partners and companions, to find our own healing as we bring healing to others.

Whenever darkness may threaten to overcome us, the Holy One is by our side. In God's light, we can face our fears and embark on future adventures. In God's love, we find healing and support the healing of others. Let us raise the light and heal the world. We are walking in the light of God!

Notes

Chapter 1: Raising the Light

[1]Bruce G. Epperly and Lewis D. Solomon, *Mending the World: Spiritual Hope for Ourselves and Our Planet* (Philadelphia: Innisfree, 2002).

[2]Abraham Joshua Heschel, *God's Search for Man* (New York: Farrar, Straus, and Giroux, 1955), 51.

[3]Charles Hartshorne, *The Logic of Perfection* (LaSalle, Ill.: Open Court, 1962), 203.

[4]Abraham Joshua Heschel, *Man Is Not Alone: A Philosophy of Religion* (New York: Farrar, Straus, and Young, 1951), 241, 242.

[5]Lawrence Kushner, *The Way into the Jewish Mystical Tradition* (Woodstock, Vt.: Jewish Lights, 2001), 156.

[6]Martin Buber, *Tales of the Hasidim: The Later Masters* (New York: Schocken, 1948), 62.

[7]Ibid., 213.

[8]Kushner, *Way,* 134.

Chapter 2: Healing for the Whole Person

[1]J. W. Provonsha, M.D., "The Healing Christ," *Current Medical Digest* (December 1959): 3.

[2]Among the most important texts in this area are the following: Herbert Benson, *Timeless Healing* (New York: Scribner, 1996); Larry Dossey, *Healing Words* (San Francisco: Harper, 1993); Harold Koenig, *Is Religion Good for Your Health?* (New York: Haworth, 1997); id., *The Healing Power of Faith* (New York: Simon and Schuster, 1999); Jeff Levin, *God, Faith, and Health* (New York: John Wiley, 2001); Dale Matthews, *The Faith Factor* (New York: Viking, 1997).

[3]Benson, *Timeless Healing,* 177.

[4]O. Carl Simonton, Stephanie Matthews Simonton, and James Creighton, *Getting Well Again* (Los Angeles: J.P. Tarcher, 1978).

[5]Martin Seligman, *Learned Optimism* (New York: Pocket Books, 1998).

[6]Allan Luks, *The Healing Power of Doing Good: The Health and Spiritual Benefits of Helping Others* (New York: Fawcett Columbine, 1991).

[7]The most extensive discussions of the role of faith as a positive factor in facing interpersonal and health crises are found in Harold Koenig's *The Healing Power of Faith* and *Is Religion Good for Your Health?*

[8]Thomas Oxnam, et al., "Lack of Social Participation or Religious Strength and Comfort as Risk Factors for Death After Cardiac Surgery in Elders," *Psychosomatic Medicine* 57 (1995): 5–15.

[9]Benson, *Timeless Healing,* 27–33.

Chapter 3: Prescriptions for Wholeness

[1]For a more extended discussion on the spiritual aspects of pain and suffering, see Bruce G. Epperly and Lewis D. Solomon, *Mending the World: Spiritual Hope for Ourselves and Our Planet* (Philadelphia: Innisfree Press, 2002).

[2]David Mahoney and Richard Restick, *The Longevity Strategy: How to Live to Be 100 Using the Brain-Body Connection* (New York: J. Wiley, 1998), 84.

[3]Norman Cousins, *Anatomy of an Illness as Perceived by the Patient: Reflections on Healing and Regeneration* (New York: Norton, 1979).

[4]Martin Buber, *Tales of the Hasidim: The Early Masters* (New York: Schocken, 1947), 102.

[5]Rabbi Nachman, *Rabbi Nachman's Stories,* trans. Aryeh Kaplan (Brooklyn: Breslov Research Institute, 1983), 354–437.

[6]Gail Warner with David Kreger, M.D., *Dancing at the Edge of Life* (New York: Hyperion, 1998), 77, 86.

[7]James Lynch, *The Broken Heart: The Medical Consequences of Loneliness* (NewYork: Basic Books, 1977).

[8]Stewart Wolf and John Bruhn, *The Power of the Clan: The Influence of Human Relationships on Heart Disease* (New Brunswick, N.J.: Transaction Publishers, 1993), vii.

[9]Lynch, *Broken Heart*, 4–8.

[10]Lawrence Kushner, *The Way into the Jewish Mystical Tradition* (Woodstock, Vt.: Jewish Lights, 2001), 102.

[11]Buber, *Tales of the Hasidim*, 212–13.

[12]Rabbi Simkha Weintraub, ed., *Healing of Soul, Healing of Body* (Woodstock, Vt.: Jewish Lights, 1994), 13.

[13]Nachman, of Breslov, *Rabbi Nachman's Tikkun* (Monsey, N.Y.: Breslov Research Institute, 1982), 41–81; Weintraub, *Healing of Soul*.

Chapter 4: From Burnout to Blessing

[1]The term "attitudinal healing" comes from the work of psychiatrist Jerry Jampolsky, author of books such as *Love Is Letting Go of Fear* (Milbrae, Calif.: Celestial Arts, 1979) and *Teach Only Love* (NewYork: Bantam, 1983), and spiritual guide Susan Trout, author of *To See Differently* (Washington D.C.: Three Roses Press, 1990).

[2]Patricia Adams Farmer, *Embracing a Beautiful God* (St. Louis: Chalice Press, 2002).

[3]Krista Kurth and Suzanne Adele Schmidt, *Running on Plenty at Work: Renewal Strategies for Individuals* (Potomac, Md.: Renewal Resources, 2003).

Chapter 5: The Healing God

[1]Abraham Joshua Heschel, *Between God and Man: An Interpretation of Judaism from the Writings of Abraham Joshua Heschel*, ed. Fritz A. Rothchild (NewYork: Harper and Row, 1959), 123–24.

[2]Mishnah, *Sanhedrin* 6:5

[3]*Midrash Rabbah on Exodus*, trans. S.M. Lehrman (London: Soncino Press, 1959), 29:1, 337. Quoted in William E. Kaufman, *Journeys: An Introductory Guide to Jewish Mysticism* (New York: Bloch Publishing, 1980).

[4]Abraham Joshua Heschel, "The Mystical Element in Judaism" in *The Jews: Their History, Culture, and Religion*, ed. Louis Finkelstein (NewYork: Jewish Publication Society, 1960), 2:950.

[5]*Genesis Rabbah* 3:9

[6]Alfred North Whitehead, *Religion in the Making* (New York: Macmillan, 1926), 152.

[7]Quoted in William E. Kaufman, *The Evolving God in Jewish Process Theology* (Lewiston, N.Y.: Edwin Mellen Press, 1999), 45–46.

[8]Denise Dombkowski Hopkins, *Journey Through the Psalms* (St. Louis: Chalice Press, 2002), 45–46.

Chapter 6: Walking in the Light of God

[1]This story was related to Bruce Epperly by the Rev. Kwame Osei-Reed.

Printed in the United States
21876LVS00003B/118-510